La Lucci

BOOKS BY SUSAN LUCCI

La Lucci
All My Life

La Lucci

SUSAN LUCCI

WITH LAURA MORTON

BLACK STONE PUBLISHING

Published in 2026 by Blackstone Publishing
Cover design by Kathryn Galloway English
Book design by Sarah Riedlinger

Printed in the United States of America

First edition: 2026
ISBN 979-8-8748-6828-4
Biography & Autobiography / Personal Memoirs

Version 1

Blackstone Publishing
31 Mistletoe Rd.
Ashland, OR 97520

www.BlackstonePublishing.com

To my family, my friends, and my fans
and to the love of my life, Helmut

A WORD ABOUT THE ORIGIN OF LA LUCCI

Many people credit Regis Philbin with coining my nickname, La Lucci, and while it is true that he was the first to publicly call me that, long before he and I met, I was often called to the set of *All My Children* as La Lucci by one of the producers or directors. Somewhere over the course of time, La Lucci became my moniker at our show. It wasn't until Regis began calling me La Lucci outside the set of *All My Children* that the name became well-known. Ever since then, it has stuck. It feels so natural when I hear it, whether it's from truck drivers passing by, airline personnel, diners and servers in restaurants, taxi drivers, fans at public appearances, or on the red carpet, and always in posts on my social media. It has become so synonymous with the name Susan Lucci that until they closed during COVID, Hoffman's Deli in my hometown served a La Lucci panini named after me. The Garden City Deli has an opportunity to pick up the banner by naming their Chicken Caesar Wrap, which I am totally addicted to, All My Chickens.

CONTENTS

1
Introduction

6
CHAPTER ONE:
Fire in My Belly

14
CHAPTER TWO:
A Cherry on Top

19
CHAPTER THREE:
The Warmth of a Grateful Heart

28
CHAPTER FOUR:
Working Mom

40
CHAPTER FIVE:
The Wisdom in Her Words

50
CHAPTER SIX:
Grace in Every Step

64
CHAPTER SEVEN:
Aging with Audacity

73
CHAPTER EIGHT:
Unforgettable

79
CHAPTER NINE:
From the Heart

89
CHAPTER TEN:
The Heart of the Matter

98
CHAPTER ELEVEN:
How Am I Supposed to Live Without You?

111
CHAPTER TWELVE:
There Must Be a Crack in the Universe

118
CHAPTER THIRTEEN:
The Quiet Strength Within

125
CHAPTER FOURTEEN:
The Strength of Acceptance

135
CHAPTER FIFTEEN:
After the Rain, the Sun She Shines

141
CHAPTER SIXTEEN:
Dancing in Life's Bright Moments

144
CHAPTER SEVENTEEN:
A Good Book, Like a Good Friend, Is Important to Find

158
CHAPTER EIGHTEEN:
The Importance of Play

163
CHAPTER NINETEEN:
Thank You for Asking

176
CHAPTER TWENTY:
You Don't Move On, You Move Forward

181
Letter to My Younger Self

183
Acknowledgments

185
Notes

INTRODUCTION

With my success, my first mandate is to entertain and then to inform.

—AGNES NIXON

There's a wonderful tradition in the theater where a single light bulb is left glowing when the stage is empty. This light is known as the "ghost light." It remains on for both practical and, sometimes, slightly whimsical reasons.

There's also a touch of mystery to the ghost light. I believe in mystery. I am drawn to it and am comfortable and intrigued by it. Maybe that's one reason why I chose to keep an air of mystery over my own life as I stepped into the limelight.

You see, there is another, almost poetic, reason for the ghost light. For actors like me, standing on that empty stage, with only the ghost light and no one else there, is an irresistible place to be. To dream your dreams. To belt it out. To dance as if everybody is watching you—with a fire in your belly and all your hopes coming to life.

Even when I was a little girl, I was always performing, with or without an audience. I was very big on wrapping my mother's scarves around my head, turning them into different costumes. These were inspired by the old movies I grew up watching on *The Early Show*, *Million Dollar Movie*, *The Late Show*, and, when I would sneak out of my bed at night, *The Late, Late Show*. Scarves and the sheer white curtains in our upstairs bathroom allowed me to become virtually anyone I wanted to be—a bride, an exotic princess, a first communicant. Sometimes I'd place a tiara on top of my head, pull a pair of my mother's long black or white gloves over my hands, and hold her ivory cigarette holder between my fingers as if I were Ava Gardner or Gene Tierney. My mother never smoked, but her brother-in-law, my uncle Leo, brought the cigarette holder back after World War II as a gift. My mother always encouraged me to play and explore my creativity, inadvertently fostering what would later become my passion and calling in life, while also nurturing her own need for some solitude away from her constantly performing daughter. Could I have been the only child in the world who walked around the house on my knees pretending to be blind while making a pilgrimage to Lourdes? When my mother would see me, usually while vacuuming, she would say, "Susan, stop! God is going to freeze your face like that!"

From the time I performed in *West Side Story* and other musicals during high school, I wanted to be on stage. I was a drama major in college and could not stay away. I would show up early and leave late, waiting until everybody else left. Then, I'd step on the stage, illuminated only by that magical ghost light, and . . . I'd perform. Alone. For only myself—but with big dreams of the audience I would someday stand in front of. I couldn't help but stand on that stage in the darkness, with just that single light, and perform. I didn't stand there silently, although there was silence all around me. It was such a joy being on that stage and singing lyrics that moved me, that had something to say, that allowed me to *feel* what it would be like someday when my dreams came true. And I thought they *would* come true. I believed it in every fiber of my being. It was very exciting—it was thrilling. *This* was where I belonged.

Being up there alone was also a moment that felt deeply personal, incredibly powerful, and emotional—kind of like writing this book.

Okay, so I'll admit that writing this time around has challenged me in ways I never expected. Early on, before the first word was written, I knew this book would be different from my first. It's a profound experience to dig deep and share your experiences with others. You start to ask all sorts of questions while examining yourself and your motives.

Will anyone care? Are my stories interesting? What if I share too much—or not enough?

In the past, I believe I was more reserved and cautious about exposing my emotions. But writing and editing at the same time as I was grieving the loss of my husband brought a ferocious river—make that a flood—of emotions running toward me that I never expected to experience, let alone share.

There were many days and nights during this writing process when I sat with my thoughts inviting reflection. This didn't come easily or without angst. I don't really see myself as a writer, but I am a storyteller, usually through performing, playing a part, or singing a song. In fact, the creative people I admire most are the writers, composers, and lyricists of the world.

Having said that, I have been so blessed to be surrounded by superb writers my entire career, starting with Agnes Nixon. Even as I write this, Agnes's words, which I shared with you at the top of this chapter, keep ringing in my ears. *First, entertain—second, inform.*

So, with that mantra as my North Star, I hope my collection of stories here—stories of my life experiences, both professional and personal—will fit the bill for you. Some offer a peek at my encounters backstage while waiting for the curtain to come up on me, while others pull back the curtain to share the raw truth about one of the most awful experiences in my private life. This wasn't easy; however, it is part of my story.

So why would I do this?

Good question.

I have asked myself that many, many times. I've come up with two reasons. First, *gratitude.* It has played such a big part in getting me to where I am now. My second reason is this: to have the opportunity and joy of taking my experiences and what I've learned from them and passing them forward.

Of course, with life being what it is, not all of my experiences have been filled with joy and light. As mentioned, I have always had a love of performing, singing, dancing, and theater. But the reality of loss that we, as human beings, all experience doesn't always get tied up in a neat little bow. Sometimes . . . life is just not a musical.

I always felt there was light within me, but the truth is, when I lost my husband, Helmut Huber, on March 28, 2022, I felt that light had gone out forever. I *believed* I had lost my light. There are no words to say how much I was missing him. And with that came a feeling of complete hopelessness. The encouragement to remain *hopeful* was shared with me so many times, but the only thing I truly hoped for was for Helmut to come walking through the door.

We all want to have light. And when I thought I had lost it—well, it was crippling.

Without Helmut, I felt like half a person.

When I think of Helmut, I think of light. He was the love of my life. He lit up every room he was in. And he understood the ups and downs of existence and a life lived in the spotlight. We learned that together. He was so generous and had such a big gregarious spirit. He touched everyone around him, leaving a lasting glow of love and laughter.

After he passed, I thought I'd never get my light back again. But I also knew I had to make a choice and somehow find the courage to put one foot in front of the other. It was better than lying on the floor in a puddle, completely destroyed. And for a while there, that is exactly how I felt. For a long time, nothing mattered.

After my mom lost my dad, she lived another nineteen years, all the while missing him very much. For many years, I didn't understand the look on her face as she navigated through life—that is, until I saw it on my own. That's when I realized my mother had been walking around in pain yet still putting on a happy face. She was trying to look pleasant, and I admired her for that. And I understood that need. Even so, I wanted to get to a place where I wasn't putting on the face. I actually wanted to be happy again. Or at least happi*er*.

It took some time after Helmut passed, and then I noticed there were more happy days than sad. I began taking better care of myself, my health, and my surroundings. And when I did, I started to see a glimmer of hope that maybe someday I'd once again find my light. And it became my quest.

"Maybe" slowly turned into "possibly." "Possibly" became "probably." And that made me very happy. I began to feel a freedom of spirit—and a new understanding of who I am. Of who I've always been.

Chapter One: FIRE IN MY BELLY

Every knock is a boost.

—JEANETTE LUCCI, née Granquist, my mother

My life has always been a story full of mixed messages. Some build us up and others can tear us down if we let them.

I know that I was incredibly lucky to have parents who loved me, were proud of me, and were always there for me. I'm so grateful for all that I learned from them, so I have the eyes to see and the ears to hear. I remember being five years old and sitting on the front porch with my dad when he said to me, "You see that moon up there? You can reach that high. Keep your feet on the ground and keep reaching for the stars, Susan. You can be anything you want to be. Never be afraid."

Maybe we are born with a certain level of self-motivation and spirit that drives our dreams. But I think so much of that has to do with the messages we receive, how we hear and see them, and what we do with them.

I have had many great teachers throughout my life—some were actual teachers and others were people I met through chance encounters. Some of these teachers encourage us to grow and blossom so we can become the best version of ourselves. Others, though, show us who we *don't* want to be. I've learned so much from both.

When I was twelve years old, like many kids, I rode the bus to school. I loved it. I loved everything about school. I loved riding the bus, and I loved being able to see my friends.

One particular day, however, all that changed. I got on the bus as I always had and walked to the back where my group of friends was seated. Strangely, there was no place for me to sit. I said hi to my friends, who happened to be all boys that morning. But there was one boy there, sitting in the middle, who was not part of our regular group. I recognized him from class but didn't really know him. In the moment, I didn't think much of his presence. But one thing I do recall is that this boy suddenly turned to me and said to the other boys the vilest and most personally destructive thing I had ever heard—in fact, to this day. I was so humiliated, so stunned, so completely in shock, but, most of all, hurt because the other boys started laughing. I couldn't believe it. These boys were supposed to be my friends. *What just happened?* Looking back, I suppose this was my first encounter with what betrayal feels like—and I've never forgotten it. I think this boy was trying to get in with the others, so he said something he thought would make him a big man on campus. It didn't. There was nothing for me to say. I didn't cry, but I turned around and walked away, toward the front of the bus until I found the first empty seat.

I sometimes wonder if that experience has also been a motivator for me. I had no control over what this boy said, and I did nothing to cause his awful behavior. The one thing I could control was how I responded. Thankfully, I chose not to engage. Was I right? I think so. Now, when I think about what he actually said, I realize his words were even worse than I knew at the time. I felt the insult, and the cruel humiliation that came with it. What I didn't understand was why the other boys laughed. Not one of those boys ever acknowledged what happened to me that day on the bus. But they were twelve years old too and probably didn't realize how awful his words were. The thing is, I have never forgotten the experience or what he said. Never. And I have never been able to bring myself to say his words out loud to anyone.

I'm sure many of us have endured being hurt. Some, many times over.

I learned the power of words that day. They have the capacity to create a moment and the strength to destroy a person. Looking back, if

I were a different type of girl, then maybe I would have had a snappy reply and laughed it off. But when I think about it, even to this day, what he did was a form of bullying, and what he said was so disgusting. It wasn't ongoing, but it was a moment I've never forgotten—a moment of wannabe elitism and racism, which makes me sick to my stomach.

My father, who always led by example, instilled in my brother, Jimmy, and me that you treat people the way you want to be treated. He taught us always to strive to do the right thing, even when it's sometimes a more challenging path to take. I set out to become the best version of me, so I would never be what that boy said I was.

There were times in my life when I would be reminded of that day—certainly when I was told I would probably never work in television because I was too "ethnic looking." That was something I heard a lot while growing up. My mother was aware of this, so whenever we'd watch the Miss America pageant together, she would always pick the brunette to be in the finals or become the winner. She would say things like, "Look at that girl, she is so beautiful, so exotic looking. I hope she wins. She should."

By the time most of us get to the fifth or sixth grade, we don't want to be different. We want to blend in and look like everyone else. I had olive skin, brown hair, and brown eyes. In addition, another thing that didn't work in my favor was the uniform I had to wear at our parochial grade school. Other schools had navy-blue uniforms with crisp white blouses. Ours, on the other hand, was a lifeless forest green with a Dacron blouse the dullest shade of beige. It didn't exactly bring out my best features. And . . . I had a vowel at the end of my name, which meant I didn't look like the other kids, especially in Garden City, where I grew up. Blonde hair and blue eyes were the standard, and something I would never have.

Later, when I was in college, I'll never forget overhearing a boy telling his friends he liked me.

"I'd love to take her home to meet my parents, but I can't. She's *I*-talian," he said, with an emphasis on the *I*.

Where I grew up, you could count the number of people with a vowel at the end of their name on one hand. I'd lie on my stomach in front of the TV pushing up my nose, hoping it would somehow become one of those little turned-up noses so many of the other girls had. I thought they were all so pretty.

Well, that never happened. But that's what I did.

Somehow, I think the balance my mother offered by always picking out the brunette beauties who were darker complexioned like me gave me a great deal of confidence. In addition, neighbors would ask me to sing and put me up on a table at birthday parties before the cake came out, which also bolstered my self-esteem. I was always getting a certain amount of very pleasant compliments from people, which countered the fact that I didn't look like everybody else. My mother and my grandmother encouraged me to be an individual and told me often that it is good to be different. How very lucky I was to have such wonderful, positive influences growing up.

By the time I was sixteen, I was doing plays and acting in the drama department at Garden City High School. Our school and our community were very sports oriented, and while I was lucky to learn a lot of very positive life lessons from those experiences, I also was blessed to have the most enthusiastic and inspiring drama teacher, Inez Norman Spiers. She was way ahead of her time, and very much an individual. She had red curly hair like Lucille Ball and wore green nail polish. She had a lot of experience in theater and sometimes invited amazing, seasoned actresses as guest speakers to our class, who inspired me in so many ways.

Once, Mrs. Spiers took me aside and said something I've never forgotten. If my dream was to pursue acting, she encouraged me to do it. But then, she looked at me, took a deep breath and remarked, "When you go to New York City to act, know this: Nobody is going to embrace you with open arms. The women are not going to like having you in their production. And some of the men are not going to like it either. So just know that." With those words, the seed had been planted.

I knew Mrs. Spiers was trying to prepare me for the fact that acting is a very competitive world, and if I chose to follow my dream, I could not rely solely on my looks or talent to break through. She wanted me to understand that there would be some women who might consider me a threat because of my appearance and perhaps would be jealous. Some men too. I heeded her warning that day, although as it turned out, that was not my experience.

I've often said that I feel a kind of kinship to athletes. I think actors and athletes have a lot in common—a tremendous appreciation for grit, determination, discipline, and commitment. In so many ways, both athletes and actors are their own instrument. Individual performance dictates we keep our instruments in top shape. It takes all of that to become the best of the best and to pursue a dream—a dream they probably could not imagine breathing without doing. I think about the young girl who starts off doing gymnastics when she is eight years old and wants to be in the Olympics. She says it out loud and declares this as her dream. Despite not knowing how hard she is going to have to work to get there, she is committed to doing whatever it takes. This burgeoning champion athlete can see herself on the podium receiving a gold medal. She dreams about it day and night, becoming obsessed, loving every minute. If she has a fire in her belly, the determination to succeed, she will never give up on her dream. The first time I saw Muhammad Ali, I thought the way he spoke about himself was bragging. I thought that people who bragged couldn't deliver. But Muhammad Ali was different. He owned his excellence; he did deliver. I really admired that—and him.

When I watch a performer, whether it is another actor, singer, dancer, or comedian, I see how it takes that same grit and determination to get to that place of excellence. No one thinks about the sacrifices that were made to achieve that level of expertise or the parents who drove their kids to practice, games, auditions, and performances. I always knew what I wanted to do—and I was determined to do it.

Although I grew up in an upper-middle-class family, nothing was ever handed to me. There were so many times early in my career that studio executives or agents would say to me, "You're really the whole package. You really have the 'it' factor. The only thing that might hold you back is you're not hungry enough. You don't come from the 'wrong side of the tracks.'"

Really?

I may have been shy, and I may not have spoken up, at least not then, but I didn't lack the spunk or the belief that I had exactly what it would take to make it. That perception was such a misrepresentation of who I was or how "hungry" I was.

All I could think was, *Watch me.*

Like that famous scene in *Pretty Woman*, when Julia Roberts walks into the boutique in Beverly Hills loaded with shopping bags from expensive stores the day after the sales staff at this particular store wrote her off and wouldn't wait on her, there have been many times over the years when I just wanted to say to those executives, "Do you remember me? Big mistake. Huge."

For years, my shyness held me back in ways I still think about today. When I was in my early twenties, I auditioned for the lead in an off-Broadway production of *The Tempest*. I had worked all day at *All My Children* and afterward went downtown to meet the director to do the scene. The director was young but very accomplished. He was coming off some great successes and was highly regarded. I was so happy to have this audition.

The director was great, giving me notes, working with me to get the scene right. I kept trying, but I wasn't getting it. This was unusual for me, as I typically understood scenes quickly. I must have done the scene three or four times before I knew it wasn't working. I was so frustrated with myself. I left the audition, hailed a cab, and drove two blocks away when it suddenly clicked. Finally, I understood what he wanted from me, and I knew I could do it. I wanted to go back. I wanted to tell the cab driver to please turn around. I wanted to charge into the rehearsal room and say, "I get it. Please give me another chance." But I didn't. My shyness held me back. Here it is, many years later, and I am still thinking about it. I could have kicked myself for letting my shyness get in the way that day and many other times too. I knew I was capable. I knew I had the goods. What I didn't understand, at least not then, was why I didn't have the nerve to go back.

Around ten or twelve years after I started on *All My Children*, that all changed when my agent set up a meeting with a producer for a film. It wasn't a casting call or a reading. It was just a get-to-know-you type of meeting in his office. By this time, many people, both fans and the press, were taking notice and becoming aware of my work. I was starting to transcend daytime television, so I wasn't a complete unknown. He had no clue about my work and didn't care.

He was incredibly dismissive of me. I was so angry at his treatment. How could he not be aware that I was on national television five days a week? Did he not watch television? Did he not read the trades? *All My Children* was aired in airports, hospital waiting rooms, doctors' offices, and even the windows at Macy's. Erica Kane was a busy character. I was in many scenes. I had a lot to do and cared about my work. I loved my work. I wanted to do it. And I was getting a lot of public attention for it.

At the time, I had also made several movies for television that always got tremendous ratings. In fact, there was one film, *Mafia Princess*, that beat the World Series in the ratings.

Maybe he thought that daytime was beneath him. Maybe he was doing someone a favor by seeing me. Certainly, that's what his behavior indicated. I felt embarrassed by his indifference. Even so, I wasn't going to sit there and rattle off my résumé. I wasn't going to sell myself. Instead, I defended myself. I could feel myself channeling my inner Erica—after all, she wouldn't have just sat there and taken this behavior, and I didn't either.

My blood was boiling.

Smoke was coming out of my ears.

I stood up and said, "Have you been living under a rock?"

This was a first for me. I had never behaved like this before or since during a meeting.

I turned on my heels and walked out of his office.

I was furious.

He didn't care.

And today, I can't remember his name. Maybe that is the best revenge.

However, I am grateful to him for one thing. That was the day I pushed my shyness back and my confidence forward. And it felt good. *Really* good. That was also the day I finally owned my excellence out loud. I had always believed in myself. Without that confidence, I could never have accomplished what I have. Not that I think I am in the same category as Muhammad Ali, but like him, I knew I could deliver on it. That doesn't mean I'm not deeply grateful and humble. I am. While I still struggle with my shyness, I consciously try not to let it hold me back—not anymore. Not since that day.

There is no accounting for self-motivation or what drives anybody's dreams. When you have a fire in your belly and a passion that drives you, nothing can stop you. I realized early on that life will consistently present obstacles and hurdles people have to overcome, so I learned to find my way over, under, through, or around that wall to get to the other side—a skillset that would serve me well throughout the years, no matter what life threw at me.

Chapter Two:
A CHERRY ON TOP

You can't stop the waves, but you can learn to surf.

—JON KABAT-ZINN,

Wherever You Go, There You Are

It's been fifteen years since Erica Kane and I parted ways. And so much has happened during that time. I will admit, after more than four decades on the air, I was shaken every bit as much as I was blindsided by the cancellation of *All My Children*.

To this day, I am frequently asked about what happened through social media and at live events. People want to know if the rumors are true—is the show coming back? Even now, *General Hospital* references Erica Kane as if she is a character on their show.

The cancellation of our show was such a devastating outcome for so many, from our fans to our *All My Children* family. In a way, it felt like a horrible divorce—one I didn't see coming or want. It was like *The War of the Roses*—I can still visualize myself swinging from the chandelier!

While rumors had been swirling for months about the impending cancellation, for the most part and at the time, I didn't think they were true.

I had that all wrong. The shoe—*not* a Manolo Blahnik but a heavy steel-toed boot—finally dropped when I received an unusually early morning call from Agnes Nixon. Given my shooting schedule, I was awake when she telephoned at 5:30 a.m. to tell me the news. Agnes said that her son Bobby had received a call from the network around two in the morning to let him know that the show was being canceled. Bobby was left with the terrible task of delivering that awful message to his mother.

I didn't want the news to be true. So much so, I did my best to convince myself that it wasn't really the end of the road. Of course, it was unthinkable to have a four-decade-long run, and I was and still am grateful for that long stretch of road, but it wasn't only my road I was thinking about. My heart was heavy with the knowledge that everything we had all worked for together over the years was coming to an unnecessary and unexpected finale.

My heart began to ache as I thought about how I had watched certain decisions destroy the production of our show and the lives of our cast and crew on both sides of the country—*twice*. These choices disassembled *All My Children* in New York, and then two years later in Los Angeles. Furthermore, another New York–based show, *One Life to Live*—also created by Agnes Nixon—was about to meet the same demise.

Interestingly, a week before this happened, I had just come off a nationwide book tour for my first memoir, *All My Life*. While on the road promoting my book, I encountered thousands of fans everywhere I went, of all ages and every background. Our show was a part of the fabric of so many people's lives. And as I spoke with these people, many wondered if what they were hearing, that the show was being canceled, was true. I did my best to reassure them that wasn't the case, but alas, it was.

What wasn't true was the excuse for our cancellation was due to the fans no longer being there—that people were no longer watching the show. I had just witnessed this with my own eyes in Atlanta, Cincinnati, Minneapolis, New York, and Los Angeles, as well as all over the country: Our fans showed up in the tens of thousands. In early 2025, I attended an event at the 92NY in New York City to celebrate the fifty-fifth anniversary of *All My Children* along with Kelly Ripa, Eden Riegel, Jill Larson, Judy Blye Wilson, Francesca James, Lorraine Broderick, and Jennifer Bassey, and moderated by Andy Cohen. The theater was sold out, with a line that was wrapped around the block. It was lovely to see but not surprising. *All My Children* fans were and are the most supportive group of people. How blessed we all were to be a part of such an iconic show.

Even so, I had to accept the inevitable. *All My Children* had been canceled. And that left me very sad.

Like so many actors, I wondered if I would ever work again. I was surprised by some of the emotions I felt. I found myself questioning my identity, something I had never done before. I wondered, *Who am I now? How will I move about in this world?* The whole experience was a shock to my system, one I felt for a while. As I said earlier, this was like a nasty divorce. I wasn't sure if I could move on, but I was well aware that I needed to move forward, almost instinctively at first because my pride wouldn't let me walk into a room where I thought people might feel sorry for me. At one point, I stopped and checked myself, thinking, *Now, wait a minute, whenever a recording artist takes time between albums, no one thinks they lost their voice. A good mechanic who has lost his job is still a good mechanic. Those skills don't leave us just because our circumstances change.* And with that, I did the best I could to deal with my emotions quickly.

So in the midst of the sadness and the anger and the many unanswered questions, I held on to an uplifting thought: I am *grateful*, so grateful that I have had the opportunity to play Erica Kane and to feel such appreciation from the fans. I still feel this way, even today.

One of my long-standing behaviors in life has always been to "accentuate the positive." This is just naturally who I've always been. Even though I was struggling with my feelings, I had to accept where I was.

Once I accepted that their decision was made, I needed to move forward with a positive attitude. So, after hearing the news and going through a period of loss and mourning, I began to look at the end of *All My Children* as a new beginning, maybe one full of fantastic opportunities that I might have otherwise not been given. In a way, I had been thrown out of the nest, and that meant it was time for me to fly—or at least try to.

Lucky, lucky me, just as *All My Children* was coming to an end, I met Marc Cherry.

At the time, there was a lot of chatter from fans on social media about wanting me to join the cast of *Desperate Housewives.* Marc Cherry came to the studio and was inquiring about me, but I wasn't there on that particular day. I later learned he liked my work and what he saw in me as an actress. Helmut and I arranged to meet Marc for lunch in the executive dining room at ABC. We instantly found him extremely easy to be with, very jovial, and we got along well. Marc told me he, too, had heard about this online movement that I should be on *Desperate Housewives* but wanted me to know it wasn't going to happen because the show was already done, in the can, and final.

However, Marc did mention *Devious Maids*, a new show he was working on, that he thought might have a part for me. Not long after, I was back in New York when I received a call to come to Los Angeles to read for the part of Genevieve Delatour, a wealthy socialite whom Marc described as "a cousin of Erica Kane" in Beverly Hills, whose interactions with her maid, Zoila, played by the talented Judy Reyes, were hilarious. Zoila had a lot more smarts than Genevieve.

Some people said, "WHAT? They want you to audition?" As for me, I had no qualms about flying to LA to audition for Marc Cherry. I had no problem with it. I admired and respected that this was Marc's process and completely understood his need to make sure I was right for the part and that we could work well together.

And as it turned out, the audition was so much fun! It was the opening scene from the first episode, when Genevieve is seen for the first time—under the bed! There was no bed in the room I auditioned in. But there *was* a cocktail table, so I crawled underneath the cocktail table as if it were the bed and we were off and running.

When I first read the part of Genevieve, I had no idea how her name was meant to be pronounced. Was it Gena-veeve or Gen-a-vee-ev? When I walked in and heard Marc pronounce the name Gen-a-vee-ev, I instantly knew who this woman was. I told Marc he had just told me everything I needed to know about this character. If you're going to follow Erica Kane, it had to be with Genevieve Delatour.

At the time, the pilot was part of the ABC Studios production. But the show went to Lifetime and, fortunately, became a hit around the world. After *Devious Maids* was green-lit, Helmut and I moved to Atlanta for filming. We got an apartment but still commuted back to New York whenever our schedule would allow it. Our daughter, Liza, had become a new mother, and we wanted to be there for her.

It's a wonderful thing to discover a new city together with your spouse. It was fun, adventurous. Putting together an apartment in a new city, as we had done before in Los Angeles, felt like we were newlyweds again, just starting out. There was something about it that we both really loved.

I enjoyed doing *Devious Maids* because it allowed me to stretch my wings as an actress and delve more into comedy—something I've always loved doing. I had the best time looking for the reality in each scene while also knowing it was meant to be funny. That's a very nice way to go to work every day—looking for the laughs, the humor. Plus, I got the chance to work with the most talented creative team of writers, producers, actors, and directors, including Eva Longoria. I didn't know Eva before the show. I just knew her work as an actress from *Desperate Housewives*. And she was terrific. But on *Devious Maids*, she was a director, and a very good one too.

Chapter Three:

THE WARMTH OF A GRATEFUL HEART

The more thankful I became, the more my bounty increased. That's because—for sure—what you focus on expands. When you focus on the goodness in life, you create more of it.

—OPRAH WINFREY

Throughout this book, I will talk about gratitude. Prayers of gratitude are how I begin and end each day. It sometimes surprises me, having lost my husband. I know some women might think, *Good riddance. Now I can do whatever I'd like.* But that wasn't me. There is no doubt that remaining grateful was the biggest challenge when I lost Helmut. It wasn't my need to know why. I knew God has a divine plan, I just wished this wasn't it—that Helmut had to go.

I wasn't always someone who practiced gratitude. My epiphany—the biggest turning point for me—was when we almost lost our son, Andreas, right after he was born. He entered this world on February 28, 1980, by C-section. At first, everything seemed fine. He was a little sleepier than Liza had been, but otherwise he was perfect. The only point of reference I had was when my daughter was born. Everything was picture-perfect. We spent a couple of routine days in the hospital and then took her home. I had no idea that just down the hall from the blissful nursery where she had rested, there existed an entirely different place for babies with complications. I didn't know anything about the other side of childbirth until Andreas was born.

Thirty-six hours after giving birth, a nurse came into my hospital room and announced, "Mrs. Huber, do not be alarmed." Well, I don't know about you, but whenever someone starts off a conversation like that, you can bet every warning bell in my body goes off. She explained that one of the other nurses noticed between feedings that our baby was turning blue around his mouth while drinking the supplementary water they often give to newborns. I'd later discover that it's not uncommon for babies to have an uneven complexion. So, it was amazing that a nurse noticed Andreas was turning blue just around his mouth. Something was wrong. That's when this nurse took Andreas from the main nursery to the NICU (neonatal intensive care unit). At the time, I had never heard of the NICU, let alone understood this was a very serious matter. When the nurse came back and told me they would not be bringing Andreas to me for his feeding that evening, I grew immediately concerned. She assured me he was in good care down the hallway in Nursery A.

I was recovering from my C-section and still had an IV in my arm. Luckily, the IV was on wheels. I got out of bed and ran down to that nursery as fast as my IV and I could make it. I flew down the hallway to be with Andreas. When I arrived, I realized I would not be allowed to go into the NICU right away. There were several doctors examining him, standing over his tiny six-pound body. I asked one of the nurses what they were doing, and she was kind to explain that they were trying to figure out why his mouth was blue. Unfortunately, the doctors on duty weren't sure what was causing the discoloration, so they ran a battery of tests, including a spinal tap, to help provide an answer. A spinal tap? On our newborn baby? He was just thirty-six hours old. I had no idea what I should do.

I stood there with my mind reeling, feeling utterly helpless. That's when I noticed our family pediatrician, Dr. Joseph Greensher, in the main nursery. When he left his private practice to become the head of the department at the hospital, he said to me, "Susan, if you ever need me, I will be there for you." And he was. He happened to be in the nursery where the babies were all healthy. I knew I wasn't able to go into the NICU, but when I caught a glimpse of him, I thought, *Surely, he can.*

I understood that he was busy, and I didn't want to interrupt him, so I politely asked one of the nurses to let him know I was there and wanted to speak to him if he could give me a moment. I didn't want to appear frantic, although inside I was. When he finished with the babies, he came out to greet me. I told him that my newborn son was in the NICU, and I didn't know any of the other doctors surrounding him. Dr. Greensher assured me they were all highly competent. But he could see I was anxious, worried, and concerned. As an actress, I thought I could hide those emotions better. However, as a parent, there was no getting around how I truly felt. I didn't know what was happening or why Andreas was in there. Dr. Greensher placed his hand on my arm and said, "I will find out."

When he returned, the doctor explained that our son's blood levels indicated there was reason for concern. They would need to send his bloodwork to the lab for evaluation. And, of course, this was all happening on a Friday night, which meant the lab was closed for the weekend. We would have to wait for the results. Again, he reassured me that the doctors treating Andreas were exceptional and he was in good hands. (I later learned how very right he was.) Dr. Paul Twist, a neonatologist and the head of the NICU, was with Andreas and would do the procedure. He was a very tall man who looked more like Larry Bird than a world-renowned physician. While I wasn't allowed to go into the room where they did the spinal tap, I was told Andreas wouldn't feel a thing. (Really?) I am certain that was their way of trying to comfort me, and I appreciated their efforts, but I can't imagine it was a pleasant experience for our little boy.

After the spinal tap, Andreas was placed in a silver tube that looked like a tiny space capsule, which enabled the doctors to examine his heart from every possible point of view. When they finished, they placed Andreas in an isolette and kept him in intensive care until we could get some conclusive answers. Seeing Dr. Twist holding Andreas in the palm of his hand is something I will never forget. He was such a towering man with hands like a basketball player, and Andreas was so tiny. When the team of doctors was done with their tests, it became a waiting game for answers—which, I was told, could take weeks. That wait was like going to hell and back.

Luckily, Winthrop Hospital had a number one rating in neonatology. People came from all over for the care our son was receiving. And this hospital was way ahead of its time in allowing parents to visit babies in the NICU 24/7. Before I was allowed to go inside, I had to put on scrubs like a surgeon, special gloves, and a mask. Then, I could go up to his little isolette, where there was a small porthole on the side, and place my hand on Andreas. I wanted him to feel my touch. And even though he was hooked up to wires all over his body, when I reached for him, he held my finger with his tiny hand—tight. I thought that had to be good—he felt so strong. I talked to him for hours at a time so he would know I was there and could tell how much I loved him.

The hospital allowed me to stay until we knew Andreas's diagnosis. They set up a cot in my room for Helmut as well. Five-year-old Liza drew pictures for her baby brother, which we hung up around his isolette so he could see them when he opened his eyes. I placed a pillow that played music inside with him too. I did everything I could think of to let our baby know that there was color and music and beauty in the world he was born into, and not just metal and glass and the sounds of monitors.

I spent nearly every waking moment in the NICU. I wanted Andreas to know he wasn't alone. It was awful to see my baby with wires attached to his little body. I ached with worry that his first impression of this world was of plastic and metal. I will never forget the sound of the beeping and buzzing machines that he was connected to during those horrible weeks. The doctors and nurses would say, "Mrs. Huber, you have to get some sleep." However, that was the last thing I wanted to do. I just wanted to be with our baby. In fact, what I really wanted to do was wrap him up in a swaddling blanket, unplug every wire, and take him home. Of course, I wasn't going to do that, but I sure fantasized about it. Call it a mother's instinct, but I just wanted to hold my baby and bring him home.

One afternoon, while I was talking to Andreas, Dr. Twist came up from behind me, placed his hand on my shoulder, and said, "Don't ever underestimate the power of what you are doing. Your prayers and your presence are making a difference. The sensation of your touch and the soothing sound of your voice have tremendous healing power. When you return your baby's gaze, that gives him the strength and the self-esteem to fight."

I've never forgotten his words and have clung to them many times throughout my life. Mind you, this was a secular hospital, and he was a man of science. He certainly had no idea how precious I hold my faith, nor my strong belief in the power of prayer. This man of science also gave credence to a mother's intuition to make her presence known to her baby.

"I can't believe you are saying this to me," I quietly said.

"It counts," Dr. Twist reassuringly reminded me.

While I was so grateful for his encouragement, I told him I felt like such a fool. "I never had caffeine, never drank a drop of alcohol during my pregnancy, ate all the right foods, and did everything within my power to give our child the best start in life," I cried. "Yet here I am in the NICU with a baby who might die."

As a mother, I ran every possible scenario through my mind. What had I done wrong? How could this have happened? Why was my baby so sick? I felt horrible, believing I had let my son down. I knew it was typical and quite normal for mothers to blame themselves when something like this happens. I couldn't help but feel guilty as I watched our newborn struggle.

I was reminded once again of the very powerful words Dr. Twist spoke to me: "Your son is surviving because you made him strong. When you talk to your baby and return his gaze, you are giving him self-esteem. You're giving him the strength to fight and survive."

What a spectacular man and doctor Dr. Twist was. By saying these things to me, he was giving me strength in the same way I was trying to keep Andreas strong.

When the first round of tests came back with no conclusive answers, Andreas was put through a second spinal tap and then subjected to all of the same tests he had already had. When the viral culture came back, Andreas was finally diagnosed with a terrible strain of the flu. The flu was at epidemic proportions in 1980. Tragically, quite a few babies who were exposed to the virus that season didn't make it. I continued working throughout my pregnancy, right up to my ninth month. I was completely healthy until the end of that month, when I had a bout of the flu. I nursed Andreas for the first thirty-six hours; if I was still sick, I could have passed the virus on to him. Luckily, my son's exposure was minimal. And happily, we now had an answer—it was treatable, and he would be okay.

During this entire time, hoping and praying that our newborn baby would survive, I had an additional concern weighing on my heart. Our little girl, Liza, was waiting for us to bring her new baby brother home. How could we possibly return without the baby? What would she think? How would she feel? What could we tell her so she wouldn't be afraid and disappointed?

Andreas was in the NICU for three and a half weeks. I remember thinking at the time how grateful I was for the nurse whose astute observations had literally saved my son's life. There were many times I noticed other babies whose parents didn't seem to be there when I was. I wondered if they were just coming in at different times than I was. Was there a schedule I wasn't aware of for visiting your baby? I asked one of the nurses, who explained that every family responds differently to a health crisis. Some parents won't leave their baby's side, while others can't handle seeing their newborn in such a fragile state. And some, she explained, see their sick child as damaged goods and sometimes step away.

I had to pause when I heard her say those words. That was the complete opposite of how I felt. And from what I could tell, how those incredible nurses felt too. These caretakers—the most tireless, loving nursing staff—were there morning, noon, and night, so no baby was ever alone. They took care of Andreas as if he were their own. And it wasn't just Andreas. Every baby was cared for and loved and spoken to and encouraged. There was one early morning visit to Nursery B that I will never forget. Nursery B was the intermediate nursery where he was transferred after being in the NICU and before he was released. It was around five o'clock in the morning, several weeks into his hospital stay. I walked in and found a nurse holding Andreas in her arms. He was swaddled, and his little feet were sticking out of the bottom. He had on tiny cowboy boots, which the nurse had crocheted. She was singing "Here Comes Peter Cottontail" to him and another baby, whom she was wheeling in an umbrella stroller with one arm while holding Andreas in the other! I stopped cold in my tracks. I was in awe of this woman and so very grateful to her. And grateful to God that my baby had survived. I don't know how nurses do the work they do. I imagine there must be a tremendous rate of emotional burnout for neonatal nurses because they are caring for very ill newborns. They cared for my son and all the babies in the nursery because those infants were in need of their love, attention, compassion, and care. They weren't doing this because they recognized me from television. It was just who they were.

I had only written one fan letter in my life, and it was to the nurses who cared for Andreas. I needed them to know how much I appreciated everything they did for us. I will never be able to truly put into words how thankful I am for the work they do for all families, but especially for the comfort and kindness they showed my family in our desperate time of need.

This wouldn't be the last time I would come to appreciate the love and care doctors and nurses provide in crisis, but it was the start of seeing everything just a little differently after that. Once I was able to bring Andreas home and was absolutely certain he'd be okay, I spent every moment counting my life's blessings. And there have been many. From that time, experiencing such kindness, regard, and expertise made me aspire to be more like them. I realized that caring and living with empathy and compassion mean so much more than possessions, fame, or fortune. I was so close to losing the things that meant so much to me.

Not long after COVID, I visited that NICU again, and to my surprise, one of the nurses who treated Andreas was still there. And she remembered Andreas, Helmut, and me. I could hardly believe it. I got to say thank you to her in person. I saw the babies in their isolettes and heard the unforgettable sounds of the monitors, and I couldn't help but think of the tumultuous time these babies were going through. My heart went out to those parents as they hoped and prayed for their babies' survival, just as Helmut and I had.

As I mentioned at the start of this chapter, I begin each day with prayers of gratitude, acknowledging how grateful I am. I don't write in a gratitude journal, but I thank God and recognize that every day is a blessing. And I've had so many blessings in my life.

When I finally won the Emmy Award, and later my Lifetime Achievement Emmy, it was necessary for me to start both speeches by saying thank you. I recognized the blessings—the blessings of having parents who loved me and let me know it every day. For parents, who valued education and who also valued me; the blessings of having such great teachers along the way who encouraged me to dream my dreams and go after them; the blessing of having the talent that I was given and all that came with it; and the blessings of having such tremendous love in my life—from my husband, my parents, my beloved grandmother, my children and grandchildren.

I am so grateful.

I've never once taken any of it for granted. When I look around at all that's happening in the world today, just having a roof over my head, a warm bed to sleep in, and food on the table, well, there is so much to be grateful for. And I want to give back. It's one of the reasons I chose to write this book. I know my experiences are similar to those so many other people are enduring or have already gone through. If sharing my story somehow helps you feel you're not alone, then I will have done something good.

While I don't write in a gratitude journal, I do read as much as I can about whatever topic interests me. When it comes to gratitude, I have devoured three books by Emily Silva. *Moonlight Gratitude, Sunrise Gratitude,* and *Find Your Glow, Feed Your Soul.* It is amazing to me that the three books I admire most on this subject were all written by the same author. These three little gems helped me a great deal. Each spoke to me, and I've found myself going back to them, reading each again, and finding new nuggets of inspiration every time.

Chapter Four: WORKING MOM

I am a work in progress, but I aim to be present. When I am at work I focus on work, when I am home I focus on family. I prioritize and I delegate. My husband makes a really good partner—we divide and conquer.

—SARA BLAKELY

Truth be told, I believe that all mothers work, whether they stay at home, work outside the home, or do a combination of both. I have a friend who has a theory that life-altering changes happen for women somewhere between the ages of twenty-seven and twenty-eight. When she shared this with me, I paused for a moment to consider where I was during that year of my life. (Makes you think, right?)

I had found out that I was pregnant with my first child when I was twenty-six. Helmut and I were absolutely over the moon with joy. I was just about to enter my fourth month and was feeling good. There had been no issues at all, so we planned a trip to the Bahamas. The doctors thought it would be fine, and as they said, I was out of the woods and could travel.

We were nestled in the Bahamas, enjoying a few days of rest and relaxation when I started to have some bleeding.

Immediately, my alarm bell went off.

Before I knew what was happening, I was doubled over in pain. It all came about so quickly. It was early morning, and I found myself wanting to lie on the cold tiles of the bathroom floor. And so, I did.

Helmut was really concerned. There was a flu going around, and we both thought this was probably what I had. I had entered my second trimester. All of the experts tell you if you get there, you're on your way to a healthy pregnancy. I didn't imagine for a moment that I was having a miscarriage.

I just wanted to be alone—hoping and praying this would pass. I suggested to Helmut he go hit some golf balls. I thought if I could just lie on those cold tiles long enough, I'd be okay. Of course, I had to convince Helmut to leave. He was reluctant, but I think he could tell I just needed some space.

An hour later, he came back to the room, and I was in really bad condition. The pain was excruciating—and getting worse.

Helmut called the concierge of our hotel, who recommended a doctor we could see right away. We were in the waiting room for quite a while. There were a few mothers with their children there too, so I wasn't sure if this was a family doctor or an ob-gyn. I didn't want to show the pain or discomfort I was in, as I didn't want to scare the children, so I tried my best to hide it.

When I was called in to see the doctor, he knew right away what was happening. Deep down, I think Helmut and I did too. The doctor recommended I have a D&C, also known as dilation and curettage.

We were sent to the Princess Margaret Hospital, a pink stucco building where they performed the procedure. I stayed overnight and was back at the hotel the next morning. Later that day, I told Helmut I just wanted to go home. We flew back to New York on what was quite possibly the bumpiest flight I had ever experienced. The turbulence was so bad that I remember thinking if I hadn't already had a miscarriage, I certainly would have had one then.

When we arrived back in New York, I thought I was fine with what happened. There was a physical recovery, but what I wasn't prepared for was the emotional recovery of this loss. My niece Monica, who is the coolest girl I know, called to see how our trip was. I told her what happened, and when I did, I found myself feeling really emotional. It felt like I had lost a baby, even though the baby wasn't born yet. To me, this was my child.

Many times I'd heard other women say they'd had a miscarriage, but back then, nobody ever talked about the emotional toll, the real sense of loss, or the grief. As I healed both physically and emotionally, there were a few occasions when it felt appropriate to talk about it during an interview or two, but nobody ever picked up on it or wanted to have a more in-depth dialogue about something so many women go through.

I needed a little time to mourn our loss and go through the grieving process, as I'm sure so many other women who have lost a baby do. It was a very emotional time. I would cry so easily and seemingly out of the blue. That kind of grief just takes you over sometimes.

While I struggled with *why* I miscarried, wondering if I had done something wrong or whether I should have kept working, I was not deterred from pursuing my deep desire to have another baby. And it didn't take us long to fulfill that dream. Joyfully, I was twenty-seven years old when I was pregnant with Liza, our firstborn. It was as beautiful an experience as could be. I worked until I was nearly nine months pregnant. Once I started to show, the writers came up with a storyline where Erica became so distraught from having *her* miscarriage, she was eating herself into oblivion. There were scenes where she ate candy and bread in bed—not necessarily at the same time, but carbs had become her comfort as she struggled with her depression. So I wouldn't appear pregnant, the crew carefully set me up under the bed covers with empty candy boxes strewn all around me. (They were happy to eat all the candy!)

Liza was born in February 1975, just a couple of months after my twenty-eighth birthday. (So you might say my friend's theory is right because that certainly was a year that had the greatest impact on me after all!) I gave birth to Liza via an emergency Cesarean, which wasn't planned but necessary. The umbilical cord had wrapped around her neck, and after twenty-two hours of labor, the doctor said he was going to do a C-section.

When we brought Liza home, Helmut and I were on cloud nine. I found myself holding her in my arms, dancing around the house, taking her from window to window, showing her the trees, the grass, the blue sky, and the infinite promise of a life to be well lived. I was overjoyed being her mommy and couldn't have been more excited to welcome this beautiful (and I mean absolutely gorgeous) baby into our lives.

I finally had a baby girl—every mother's dream, or at least it was my dream. I could dress her up in beautiful clothing, and I could teach her everything I wanted her to know. I was the youngest child in my family—my brother, Jimmy, was six years older—so I hadn't had any experience caring for an infant until Liza. Even when I babysat as a teenager, it was for children, not babies.

Becoming a mother awakened a profound sense of gratitude unlike anything else I had ever experienced. It was the realization that life has entrusted you with the precious gift of nurturing this little human from its very beginning. Every tiny milestone—the first smile, the first steps, the whispered "I love you"—became a reason to be thankful. Gratitude blossomed in the quiet moments too: rocking my sleepy child, feeling her tiny fingers wrapped around mine, or hearing her laughter fill the room—or later, hearing her as a toddler singing as she was running down the hallway. Even in the challenges, motherhood teaches resilience and unconditional love, deepening appreciation for the journey. It's a constant reminder that amid life's complexities, love remains simple and infinitely abundant. It's unconditional love that is real—and exists. And it's the kind of love I always felt from my mother and was now giving to my newborn daughter. This is the truth for me: One of the greatest joys of my life is to know this kind of love that I have for both of my magnificent children, my daughter and my son.

Growing up, my mother was a stay-at-home mom and housewife. She had been an OR nurse, and then she stopped working when my brother, Jimmy, was born. Once I came along, she was well into her routine of being a stay-at-home mom.

I was not.

I worked full-time. So as a parent, I always found myself with my feet in two canoes, often pulled in polar-opposite directions because I wanted to be in two places at once. During both of my pregnancies, I worried the show might replace me or create another character that everybody would think was better than mine, and my lifelong dream of being an actress would come to an end. But that didn't happen. In fact, after Andreas was born, the writers made a mistake and wrote me back into the show a week early. On top of that, when I read the first script, it said, "Erica appears in a sexy tight nightgown." WHAT?!!!

I didn't have a chance to lose all the weight I wanted to lose before going back to work—and now I had a week less to do it! So, I ate a lot of asparagus that week!

Did I ever feel guilty? Sometimes—okay, maybe a lot of times. I never wanted my children to miss out on anything simply because I wasn't home all the time. When I went back to work after taking a few months off for maternity leave, I would call home every free moment I had during the day. The directors made so much fun of me, asking, "What is she saying to you? She's just a few months old!"

Of course, she was four months old, so she wasn't talking. But I could hear her breathing, and I could speak to her, and she could hear my voice, so that was good in my mind. We were not allowed to have a phone in our dressing rooms at the time. (There were only landlines back then.) So any chance I had during the day to slip into a control booth or an executive's office and call, I'd take it. Once, during lunch, I went into the office of Bob Iger, who was the studio supervisor for our show back then. (Of course, today he is the CEO of the Walt Disney Company.) Obviously, this was very early in his career. I asked him if it would be okay if I used his phone. He was always so nice and very elegant, and he said yes.

There were days when I had a late call time in the morning or when I finished up early enough to either take or pick up the children from school. These are fond memories. And I never missed a dance recital, school play, big game, or golf tournament. My family was and always will be my first priority.

Shortly after Liza was born, ABC offered to write a nighttime series for me. If I chose to do it, I would leave *All My Children* and do the primetime series instead. I wanted to do it, but I knew if I agreed, I would never see Liza. Helmut and I would discuss the possibilities as they came up, but I never wanted to be away from my children. Besides, when Liza and Andreas were born, I was so very, very happy.

I threw myself into being the best mother I could be. I would put Liza to bed every night. She was our firstborn child, and everything was new to me. If she cried, I would dash into her room to see what was happening instead of letting her cry as was recommended. I had a laundry list of possible causes that ran through my mind. *Is her diaper full? Is she hungry? Is a pin from her diaper poking at her?* (Do any of you remember cloth diapers and diaper pins?) Usually, there was no reason for the crying other than babies cry. I would rub her little back until she'd fall asleep, which sometimes would take a very long time. Often, Helmut would come up behind me and place his hand on Liza's back, and we would seamlessly transition from my arms to his so I could swap out.

As she grew, I began reading to Liza, and then Liza began reading to me. I would read her *Goodnight Moon*. I would carry her to all the windows, where she would look outside and point, saying, "My moon, my moon." It made her so happy. I'd hold her in my arms and read that book over and over. I knew those were numbered days, so I soaked up every moment we shared together on those nights. When we finished reading, Liza would lie down and get comfortable under her covers. I'd turn off the light, and she would start talking to me. I would sit on the edge of her bed, rub her back as I'd done when she was a baby, and play with her hair, and she would talk to me in the dark. There is something magical about the darkness. The quietness and calmness somehow created a lovely space for Liza to tell me all about her day, her friends, her thoughts. And much to my happy surprise, as she continued to grow, our little ritual kept going. If you've raised a teenager, you know getting more than a couple of words from them can be like pulling teeth. So, when she started to talk, I listened. I gave her a forum to feel seen and heard. For me, as a mother, this was fantastic. In the dark she would tell me all about her day, what cute boy she liked, or something mean a girl had done or said to her at school.

One time, when Liza was around eleven years old, she said to me in the dark, "Mommy, I wish you were a businesswoman and not an actress." Naturally, this took me a little by surprise, and yet I wanted to explore why she felt this way. Whenever my children asked me a question, especially a difficult one, I wanted to do my best to give them an answer from my heart. I also wanted them to know that I meant what I said—that my word was my bond.

I explained that if I were a businesswoman, I'd have to take a lot of business trips and would be away from home. Sure, there were times I was away filming a movie for the week, but Helmut and I had a pact between us that we would never be apart from the children or each other for more than six sleeps. "Six sleeps" is what we used to say to the kids because it was something easy for them to count. And then, I'd be home—usually in fewer than six sleeps. When Liza talked as she did in her darkened bedroom, I felt deeply connected and like I understood what was going on with her. This wonderful ritual continued until she was in college. I kept thinking that by the time she was fifteen or sixteen it would end, but she never gave me the boot.

When my daughter went off to college, I just couldn't bear walking past her room, which was suddenly dark because she was away at school. After three nights of experiencing that absence, I walked into her room and turned the lights on. I can't really explain why, but for me, it just made such a difference in how I felt. It made me feel as if her presence were still there. And when Andreas went off to college, I did the same thing in his room. There was a certain comfort I felt when their lights were on in their bedrooms. It just made me feel better—made me feel them in the house, still close to me. And after a while, I came to feel that by turning their room lights on, somehow I was also putting a blessing on them too.

All throughout their childhood, I'd often speak with our family pediatrician, concerned about the impact my career might have on Liza and Andreas. Maybe it was my guilt, or perhaps I wanted to make sure he didn't see any signs indicating that I should quit working. And I would have in a heartbeat if that were the case. Dr. Joseph Greensher, our family pediatrician who was also the head of the practice, said to me, "Don't ever give up your dreams because you were born a female. This is what I tell my niece and daughter, who are both in med school. Your children are both fantastic. But if I ever see any reason for you to stop working, I will tell you."

Fame is not easy to manage, but believe me, your kids will keep you humble. (And you don't need to be famous to experience that, right?) It happens to all of us.

When Andreas was around three years old, we went to Lord & Taylor for lunch. One thing most of us teach our children when they're little is not to talk to strangers. During the course of lunch that day, several women came up to speak to me. When they left, Andreas asked, "Mommy, who are they?"

"They are ladies who recognized me from my work on TV," I said.

Andreas thought about it for a minute, looked at me, and gesturing with his arms, he said, "So Mommy, out of *ALL* of these people, only *four* ladies recognized you?"

Well, that surely made me laugh. Out of the mouths of babes, right?

There were so many stories I'd share with my mom about my journey in motherhood. Sometimes I'd vent, but mostly we would just laugh together. One day my mom said something to me I've never forgotten. In fact, I cherish her words to this day because they're even more meaningful to me now than when she first shared them. She said, "Someday you're going to miss all this, Susan, even the sister-brother fighting, the crazy schedules. So enjoy it while you can."

All moms juggle many emotions and are always trying to do the balancing act. Everyone is different, but for me, there was a constant tug. There were plenty of days I would think to myself, *In my next life I would like to come back as either a homebody or a gypsy, but not both.*

The reality is, I *am* both. I like being out and about, and I like being home. I like being busy. I never sit down. I love being on the move. I just wished I could also be home at the same time!

Of course, I was able to share many experiences with my children because of my career, although some took a turn I never saw coming. I brought Liza to her first concert in New York City when she was a little girl. Madonna was playing at Radio City Music Hall, and the Beastie Boys were opening for her. Before the Beastie Boys came on stage, a lot of fans at the theater recognized me. This was long before cell phones and selfies, but there were many requests for autographs. So many, in fact, that security came over to see what was happening. They held the curtain for fifteen or so minutes to get everyone where they belonged and under control, which I wasn't aware of at the time. I would never want my presence at a show to delay the curtain going up—but it did!

I was always fine with fans, but I was reluctant to sign anything when my children were with me. My first thought and instinct were to protect them. At the time, I didn't want to have my daughter frightened by the pandemonium around us. I just wanted to be with her and enjoy the show like any other concertgoer.

As my children got older, there were times when they had their own experiences with paparazzi, which I hated. Andreas was a nationally ranked junior golfer, and on several occasions he was followed by the paparazzi while playing golf. They were on a public street on the perimeter of the course, which was considered legal, so they could catch a shot of him. In general, the paparazzi were respectful when I was out with my kids, especially when they were younger, so incidents like this were hard to understand and accept as a parent. My children's safety has always been my first priority, so if I ever felt like they were being threatened or intruded upon . . . well, let's just say I didn't take it sitting down.

This is one of the reasons I am so grateful I raised my children in my hometown. It turned out to be a wonderful decision. We decided to stay in Garden City because Helmut, who was from the gorgeous Austrian Alps, thought Garden City was quite beautiful. Before we were married,

I wanted to live in Manhattan. Helmut had already been living there for ten years, so he was very happy to move to my hometown on Long Island, which had grass, trees, and charm. He would often say to me, "This is a great place to raise children. Garden City has great schools, great parks, great golf courses, and a great sense of community." Boy, did he have that right.

In my hometown, everyone had my back. If the paparazzi showed up, the butcher, the florist, and the deli and local store owners would play dumb when asked any questions. "We don't know her. She lives here?" was pretty much their standard response. Living in the town where you grew up holds a special connection that fosters a tight community bond. This came in especially handy when the kids were teenagers, going to parties and cruising around with their friends. I could call the parents of their friends, who were very likely people I went to high school with—or maybe even grammar school—and check on their stories.

"Are you sure the parents are going to be home?"

"Are you sure it's really a class trip and not just kids in your class going on a trip?"

"What time do your kids have to be home after the party?"

"Are your kids allowed to go to the beach after the prom?"

I never wanted my children to miss anything simply because I was working. I grew up in a home where my parents were always present, regardless of their commitments. They set such a fine example for me. Whenever I was in a school play or at a football game as a cheerleader, my parents were always in the audience for me, and I wanted that for my children. For the most part, my schedule at *All My Children* allowed me to be at their performances or games. But one time, I couldn't make it to a performance that Liza was in. I reached out to the school and asked if I could come to the dress rehearsal instead. To my delight, the teachers agreed. At the time, I suggested that I couldn't be the only working mother in the school body and that perhaps they could extend that opportunity to all of the working mothers (and fathers) who couldn't make that performance.

Frederica von Stade was one of the mothers there. (She is a world-renowned opera singer.) Her daughters were in between my children in age. At the Christmas concert, all the parents assembled in the audience, and there was a time to sing the Christmas songs with the children on stage. During this particular concert, Helmut and I were sitting right behind Frederica. As we were all singing, one of her daughters, who was still a young girl, turned to her mother and said, "Mommy, don't sing." As I said, our kids sure know how to keep us humble!

I played Erica Kane by day, and I would run home to make Andreas's baseball practice in the afternoon and then karate in the evening. Or when Andreas didn't have sports events going on, I would take my daughter Liza and her best friend, Katie, to dance class on the North Shore of Long Island or ice skating on Hubbell's Pond, which is close to where we lived. I wore every hat that moms typically wear. And I loved every minute of it. Looking back, I wouldn't have traded a single moment, car ride, game, or performance for anything. It was stressful, but in those moments we made some of our best memories.

I will never forget one particular time when I worked all day on *All My Children* and then got in the car so I could zoom out to our house at the beach to take my then nine-year-old son to the junior sports program dance at our club that night. As I was changing to take him to the dance, he ran into my bedroom, all dressed for the dance, and said, "Mommy, I don't know how to dance."

I said, "Oh, I'm sure you do. You have such good rhythm and you're a great athlete. I'm sure you'll be fine. But just in case, why don't you come over here and we'll give it a try." Then I reached my hand out to grab hold of his.

I quickly taught him the box step right there in my bedroom that afternoon so he would know he could do that. And he was wonderful. Then we went downstairs and got into the car. On the way to the dance, I said, "Andreas, there is one more thing I'd like you to know before you go to your dance tonight. When you ask a girl to dance, go over to her table and politely ask her if she would like to dance with you, and then take her hand to lead her out to the dance floor. And when you're finished, remember to walk her back to her seat at the table. Don't just leave her high and dry. Okay?" I wanted him to know that it is always important to be a gentleman.

"Okay, Mommy. Okay." Andreas nodded his head in agreement.

When we arrived at the dance, a dozen or so little girls were standing outside waiting for him on the front porch of the clubhouse.

"Oh, Andreas is here. Oh, Andreas is here." They were so cute as they clapped and giggled.

I smiled, dropped him off, and told him to have a great time.

A few hours later, I picked Andreas up. When he got in the car, I asked, "Andreas, how did it go? Did you remember to take the girl back to her seat at her table afterwards?" I was quizzing him like a typical mother. I couldn't wait to hear all about his night.

He said, "Mommy, it's not like that anymore. The girls asked the boys to dance!"

Well, I didn't see that coming, but I had to laugh. Times may have changed, but there is no doubt I planted the right seeds that night, as Andreas has become such a good, kind, and caring man—and a good dancer too!

Now that our children are grown and out of the house, I still feel as though I am home—even if, on occasion, I still turn the lights on in their bedrooms. I have lifelong friends in my hometown, and I find I really like that feeling of rootedness. There are still people here who remember me with my mother when I was a teenager, and those who knew my father and remember him with warmth and high regard, which makes me feel so good.

Chapter Five:

THE WISDOM IN HER WORDS

The great and the least,
The weak and the strong,
The rich and the poor,
In sickness and health,
In joy and sorrow,
In tragedy and triumph,
You are all my children.

—AGNES NIXON

I have had the great privilege of working with many great entertainers and role models throughout my career. Agnes Nixon, the creative force behind *All My Children*, was the first. Not only did she entertain and inform, she also enchanted and ensnared audiences with her brilliance, writing for decades. She opened the doors for daytime television to tackle and discuss serious and important issues and quite literally put words in my mouth for forty-one years. Agnes once said early one morning in the rehearsal hall that Shakespeare had already written all the good storylines. It was up to us—succeeding generations—to find fresh and innovative ways to tell those stories. Love and hate, jealousy and revenge, fights for power and glory. Through Agnes's brilliance and creativity, she taught me the appreciation of good storytelling.

In 1996, I had the honor of presenting Agnes Nixon with the Soap Opera Digest Lifetime Achievement award. Oprah Winfrey, Carol Burnett, Judith Light, and our show's executive producer, Felicia Minei

Behr, each paid homage to Agnes that night. You may not realize this, but Oprah and Carol were both enthusiastic fans of *All My Children* and had appeared as guests at one time or another.

I stood on the stage that evening, honoring a woman who meant so much to so many. I had worked on my speech for weeks, hoping the words I chose would reflect the depth of appreciation and respect I had for Agnes. I had awakened early that morning, quietly practicing in the bathroom of our hotel so I wouldn't wake Helmut (which I did).

So when it was showtime, I took a deep breath, turned, looked at Agnes in the audience, and began to speak:

"To quote Cole Porter, 'You've got that thing.' And the song goes on to say, 'You've got that thing that makes birds forget to sing.' Oh, you've got that thing, all right. That thing that makes people schedule their classes, their work, their vacations, the birth of their babies, their entire lives around watching your shows. Now, if I were smart, I would leave it at that, right? I mean, if Cole Porter couldn't come up with a lyric that more fully described the magic certain people have that sets them apart, then who am I? Many people stop me and ask, 'What is Agnes Nixon really like? Tell me about Agnes Nixon.' So, I'll try.

"Oh, there is magic all right. There's magic in the lady herself, and magic in her writing. I think that Agnes Nixon actually works on an additional wavelength. I mean, how else can we explain all of those incredible stories that she writes months and months before they ever appear in the headlines of our newspapers? And on a personal note, it was Agnes Nixon who predicted the birth of my first baby in real life. She predicted the exact month, the exact day, and that my baby would be a girl. She did this on her Ouija board—and I wasn't even pregnant yet.

"Well, in addition to Agnes's obvious intelligence and extremely hard work—and I mean ongoing, hands-on, creative hard work—there is her legendary sense of humor. Everyone who has ever worked with Agnes talks about it. You only have to be in her presence for five minutes to know it yourself. And besides, it shows. It shows in her writing; it's one of the things her audiences love best about her. And it shows in the gleam of her eyes. It shines from her beautiful blonde hair and blue-eyed face. And something I think would surprise a lot of people, because Agnes is such an enormous presence in this industry and has achieved such greatness, she is a perfect size four. I mean, maybe I am guessing, and it's a perfect size two. But in any case, Agnes Nixon has more style in her little finger than most of us could ever hope to have in our entire being in our entire lifetime. Agnes . . . I want your clothes.

"Finally, there is one more thing that I'd like to say about Agnes. It's a word that isn't heard very often. Agnes has grace. Grace in the way she walks, grace in the way she talks, grace in the way she deals with the enormous demands of her career, grace in the way she keeps her family close, grace under pressure. Grace in how she writes her stories, how she weaves and interweaves her plots. Agnes, on behalf of everyone at home watching you tonight and every day, and on behalf of all of us in this room tonight, especially those of us who have been lucky enough to be handed one of your timely and timeless scripts, thank you for gracing us with your presence."

A few days later, I received a note from Agnes in the mail. Throughout the years, Agnes and I often corresponded with one another. Mind you, this was well before email and texts, so letters in the mail were how we expressed our feelings and fondness for each other. (And who doesn't love getting letters in the mail—even now?)

Dearest Susan,

What an embarrassing situation; a writer at a loss for words! But that is my predicament in trying to thank you for your words at the Soap Opera Digest awards. You were so magnanimous, so gracious and so beautiful in your calla lily satin sheath, that I was truly overcome and the tears started. As a result, my contact lens came dislodged and if Keith HC hadn't been there to take my arm, I'd probably had fallen up the stairs.

Naturally, I watched the show later on tape and the thought struck me how unique our relationship is! Surely one that could only have happened until our current second half of the century. Certainly over the ages, writers have had their favorite stars for whom they write; but has there ever been a writer who conceived a part from her own childhood and then passed the character on to an actress of another generation who, during the next quarter of a century, made that character develop, grow, mature, teach and entertain quite as much as the creator of the first part? And without ever brainstorming together!! There's something metaphysical about it, which perhaps Fra now understands.

Anyway, I am humbly grateful for it all and love you quite as much as Erica. Thank you again.

Agnes
2/21/96

There were so many times I'd open an envelope from Agnes and would be struck at how profound her insights were and always how thoughtful. Remarkably, Agnes intuitively had the right words at the right time, which was and still is very meaningful to me. So much so, I kept her letters as keepsakes. Sometimes they were quick thank-you notes for sending flowers or for dinner. Other times, she would congratulate me on a promotional appearance or my performance during a specific show. And many, many, *many* times, she wrote of her disappointment in my not being awarded an Emmy:

My Dearest Susan,

Of all the injustices yesterday, the one against you makes the rest pale by comparison. I realize that no words of mine can lessen the dismay, pain and fury—nor should they—but I did want you to know that I am living through those emotions with and for you.

I seldom pray for things so material as winning an Emmy but this year it did not seem im-material and I unabashedly petitioned "Let Susan Win. Above all, let Susan win." (In sober truth, those were my words and sentiments.)

Well, my prayer wasn't answered but one can't blame God for the stupid anachronistic compilation of the "Blue Ribbon" panel. We have long known what a travesty it is but even with that knowledge, I'm aware from long personal experience, does not lessen the hurt.

The only consoling thought I can think to offer you is that, thank God, you have another life—a wonderful personal one—to mitigate the sting of the professional one and secondly, that, for whatever it's worth, you are my Star of Stars, and have the highest award in my own Hall of Fame.

With deepest gratitude for your great talent and immense professionalism—and with much love—

Aggie
6-11-1982

Agnes always wrote her letters with the same passion and expression as she did our scripts. These letters were straightforward and straight from her heart. And they were absolutely filled with the kind of unparalleled love and support anyone could ever ask for. Knowing that Agnes took the time to extend her wisdom, her grace, and her gratitude deeply touched me. I was the one who was grateful to *her* for creating the spectacular, fabulously flawed Erica Kane—and entrusting me with playing her! Agnes's words to me were so generous and warm, but truly, everything I needed to play Erica Kane to the hilt, I saw in the words Agnes wrote on the page. How lucky was I to be the one Agnes told her stories of love and glamour and passion and humor and humanity through!

The first time I met Agnes Nixon was twenty-six years before the night *Soap Opera Digest* honored her with that Lifetime Achievement Award. It was during my fifth callback for the part of Erica Kane. The producer was talking to me when I glanced over and saw her. He must've noticed me looking her way.

"That's Agnes Nixon," he said.

There she was—this petite, blue-eyed, blonde standard of beauty, wearing a cocoa-brown Yves Saint Laurent pantsuit. I didn't know it was Agnes until he mentioned it. It was the first time I had ever seen a professional woman—or any woman—in such designer clothes in action and in person. I only recognized the suit because it was in the fashion magazines I had read in college, and I had just recently graduated.

This is the woman who had created the show and who had written the very scene I was about to audition with—a knock-down, drag-out fight between a spirited fifteen-year-old Erica Kane and her much more sensible mother, Mona, played by the wonderful Frances "Fra" Heflin. The mother-daughter stories I had seen on TV growing up were always so reverential, like greeting cards, but this was realistic and, in its way, revolutionary, like so much else that Agnes introduced to television.

I was cast as Erica Kane in 1970, the same year *All My Children* made its debut on ABC. This was shocking. I'd been told that I would probably never work in television because I was too ethnic looking. If only I had blonde hair or at least blue eyes. And yet, Agnes, who was indeed a blue-eyed, blonde classic beauty, chose me. I'm told that when she saw me on camera for the first time, she said, "Those are Erica's eyes."

Looking back, it was clear that Agnes had a vision for Erica from the start. The mere notion that she saw Erica's eyes in mine was bold for the time. My look was not what America saw as mainstream. Agnes wasn't concerned about that. She wanted something different. Everything changed after our fateful meeting on that day.

From the first script, I knew Erica was a one-of-a-kind character. She was passionate and tempestuous and drove men wild. She got away with saying and doing things that other women only wish they could say and do. Men wanted to either kiss her or kill her. Or both. She was the result of a truly collaborative effort between Agnes Nixon and, as she so generously said, me.

As I said, when I first started playing Erica, she was a fifteen-year-old high school girl. One day there was a scene in a coffee shop, where I was sitting in a booth. In rehearsal, I remember asking if it would be okay if I could change my hairdo? In my mind, Erica was the kind of girl who got a hall pass and, in between classes, went to the girls' room and changed her hair, put on some lipstick, and came out looking—well, different. She wasn't a very secure person. Her looks were her primary focus.

It was very rare for me to make any suggestions, and that was pretty early on. It was an organic request that came from the character I was still creating and developing. For the most part, I was terrified to speak. I was shy. However, I somehow always found the courage to say something if I strongly believed in it.

Thankfully, the producers loved the idea, and the adult actresses on set were extremely supportive. So, this was the beginning of collecting moments that would change my trajectory. They gave me strength, courage, and the ability to trust my instincts.

What made Erica Kane such a one-of-a-kind character was that she was the result of a truly collaborative effort. Agnes graciously shared with me many times over the years that Erica was as much mine as she was hers. I must confess that I often thought Erica and I were extremely lucky to have been put into Agnes's very fine and caring hands from the beginning. Day after day, for four decades, what I saw on the page took my breath away. Agnes once described Erica's spirit as a phoenix rising from the ashes. She could not be kept down for very long. With Agnes's writing and a tremendous amount of trust and camaraderie among the cast, I was able to continuously take risks as an actress and really spread my wings and fly. What a gift.

Agnes continued to be my champion, writing me notes to assure me I was doing a good job with the character. She made it easy with her writing and insights. Even so, I always appreciated hearing her perspective, which she was happy to share. Below is a note I received from Agnes after a scene I did with my "brother" on the show, who had a drug addiction. The scene revolved around a family intervention.

Dear Susan,

I must give expression to my admiration of your performance on today's air show during Mark's intervention (rather your intervention on him!)

You were quite simply superb. Not that you haven't been superb before this time you had a script and subject which allowed your talent a different range and you had this fan in tears! And shouting, Bravo!

I do hope you will sincerely consider today's scene—plus the upcoming ones in the family therapy session for the next Emmy Awards. I'm sure you cringe at the word as much as I do but you really must not let such an epiphany of talent go unnoticed.

And on a much more personal note, thank you for delivering a message from our family to the American people.

Best Love,

Aggie

All My Children aired its final episode on September 23, 2011—forty-one years after I was cast in the role—and I still find myself looking back on those years with such love. Sure, it was wonderful to have a steady acting job, and I adored the people I worked with. However, it was the relationship I forged with Agnes, and ultimately Erica—and the fans—that really gave me so much more than I could have ever dreamed of. Through her, I gained confidence in myself—as both a woman and an actress. I learned the value of being in good hands—something I will talk about a lot in this book.

Of course, I went through a period of mourning after *All My Children* was abruptly canceled. In so many ways, this was an unexpected loss. And like any loss, there was a period of denial, anger, and *eventually*, acceptance.

Agnes Nixon passed away on September 28, 2016, in Haverford, Pennsylvania. Her death came after complications from Parkinson's disease, and she succumbed to pneumonia.

For the Daytime Emmys in 2017, I was asked to speak about Agnes and pay tribute to her in memoriam. It was an honor for me to remember Agnes and all of her contributions to television and to my life and to the lives of so many others, especially among my peers and members of her family who were there that night.

Agnes Nixon was a visionary. She was a fearless and triumphant storyteller. She was not content only to imagine and create characters and stories. She had the courage and determination to get them onto network television. Agnes was also a pioneer, using her successful shows to start conversations about drugs, transgender issues, homosexuality, the Vietnam War, and interracial relationships, just to name a few. All of this with characters at a time when none of these issues were being portrayed on television—day or night. Agnes wrote stories long before they appeared in headlines or primetime. I've been told my character, Erica, was the first character on television to have a legal abortion—not Bea Arthur as Maude. Agnes Nixon had a double dose of storytelling DNA: her Irish ancestors, whom she spoke of with such affection and gratitude for their inspiration, plus she grew up in the South surrounded by its great traditions of storytelling. It's safe to say that Agnes has touched the lives of millions of viewers and the lives of so many people in television.

No matter how successful Agnes was in her career, she never lost sight of her focus, which was her family. Toward the end of her life, Agnes became a little fragile physically, having battled Parkinson's disease and then a stroke, but she still remained the youngest mind in the room.

We would go out to dinner, and she would be wearing one of her Pucci dresses, looking fabulous. She had a little trouble walking, but she did walk. She had a little trouble speaking, but she kept on telling her stories and her jokes. The spunk—the spirit she had throughout her life and career—never left her. Just days before her passing, she had finished writing her memoir, *My Life to Live*, which detailed her remarkable career in television and her personal journey. She did what she loved doing most and wrote to the very end. The night before she died, she asked her son Bob to read and reread the book jacket copy from her memoir one more time, so she could sign off on it.

Anyone who knew Agnes loved this warm and brilliant, gracious and inclusive woman. I am so proud to say that Agnes Nixon was my friend. She was my mentor in every way. She was someone I looked up to and someone I treasured.

I love you, Agnes.

Chapter Six:
GRACE IN EVERY STEP

The women whom I love and admire for their strength and grace did not get that way because s— worked out. They got that way because s— went wrong, and they handled it. They handled it in a thousand different ways on a thousand different days, but they handled it. Those women are my superheroes.

—ELIZABETH GILBERT

When I first started writing the chapter on Agnes Nixon, I had intended it to be about many of the women whom I greatly respect, from Sophia Loren to Elizabeth Taylor, two phenomenal actresses and great beauties I admired growing up. I have had the great privilege of meeting so many interesting, brilliant, wise, and generous women throughout my life, each of whom have had some indelible impact on me. There were so many who were incredibly kind and encouraging to me over the years.

I also had the extraordinary opportunity to work with many talented actors, actresses, and creatives. When I first started on *All My Children*, I spent a great deal of time watching and learning from these seasoned professionals. There were four of us playing high school kids, just starting out in our careers, while everyone else on the show was really experienced. We used to have to come in the day before and rehearse at a nearby apartment building. ABC rented a place close to the studio for that purpose. After we did a table read, the "kids" were kept there to run the scenes. So we learned a lot, whether it was from observing the other actors or listening to the notes we received. I also learned from the other actors' responses to their notes. And I certainly learned from the directors.

I particularly learned from observing Fra Heflin, who played Mona, Erica's long-suffering mother, on *All My Children*. I'd listen to her tell stories about working with Charles Laughton on stage in London. Her heart and her home were always open to me, and she, like Agnes, had a delicious sense of humor. And, I also learned from Eileen Herlie, who played Myrtle Fargate. Before joining our cast, she had worked with Laurence Olivier, playing his mother in *Hamlet*, although she was too young to play his mother. She was such a great character actress, it didn't matter. She was a professional through and through, so real and warm. Ruth Warrick, who played Phoebe Tyler Wallingford, was another great teacher. She had come from the legendary Mercury Theatre, where she worked with Orson Welles! Ruth was very glamorous and yet so down to earth. She was also good at giving advice—more about life than acting. Sometimes I would sit on the couch in the Wallingford living room or the Tyler living room, and Ruth would share her seasoned wisdom about men and children and so much more—and I would soak it all up. What an opportunity! It was fantastic. I remember she once said that every woman should have a three- or four-year-old son in her life because a little boy at that age just adores his mother. I had no children yet, so I didn't really understand what she meant. But when my little boy was three or four years old, I certainly knew exactly what she meant. And even though she had been married several times, I found her advice about men fascinating and insightful. It was such fun to listen to her. Even then, I recognized the gift of these professional relationships and was thankful for the chance to learn from these iconic actors.

I was so encouraged by the more senior actresses. It was something of a revelation for me because my acting teacher in high school had warned me that I would encounter jealousy as I embarked on my career, especially from other women. When I was growing up, there wasn't a girl power movement yet. Women were envious of each other. *Catty* was the word most often used to describe the behavior. At least that is what I was told, and there was a certain amount of truth to that, depending on the situation, but I never felt any type of animosity from those senior actresses on our show—even when my career was taking off and I started getting a lot of attention.

Aside from Agnes Nixon's incredible writing, there were several other talented writers who crafted the various storylines on *All My Children* over the years. One of those writers was Lorraine Broderick. Lorraine Broderick's career has spanned decades, during which time she established herself as a master of emotionally rich, socially relevant, and character-driven storytelling. She was mentored by Agnes Nixon, and they were quite a formidable team.

Lorraine began her tenure at *All My Children* as a scriptwriter in the late 1970s and later became the head writer during several periods throughout the show's run. Agnes insisted on addressing issues such as racism, abortion, LGBTQ+ rights, and AIDS and fought to get them on the air—in some cases for years. Each of these compelling, often groundbreaking storylines were handled with exceptional sensitivity and nuance. In doing so, Agnes, as creator, and Lorraine, as head writer, crafted some of the most memorable narratives on television and developed rich, multidimensional roles for the actors on our show, including me. And I remain so very grateful for their care and talent.

Both Agnes and Lorraine were never shy about sharing how they felt about my work. Whether I won an Emmy or lost an Emmy (and there were lots of the latter), or they were commenting on certain storylines they were writing, both sent me the kindest, most supportive handwritten letters, which I've treasured for years. The highest praise any actor can hear from a writer is how much they appreciate what you've done with their words. Here are a few notes from Lorraine:

May 17, 1988

Dear Susan,

Congratulations again! This was an outstanding year for you and I truly hope you'll finally be honored as you deserve for your incredible contribution to Daytime.

I know it will be hard to select material this year because there was so much that was good but I do remember being especially moved by the scene in the hospital in which you learned that your baby might be in jeopardy. The scenes were with Joe—you begged him not to let your baby die and I was in tears. Your performance was so powerful and so moving. I really miss working on the show and hope this awful strike is over soon. In the meantime, I look forward to your nighttime movie (thank heavens ABC finally came through with something!) It was also delightful to see you back on the show last week—you were sorely missed.

Once again, many congratulations and I look forward to seeing you and cheering for you on June 29th.

Sincerely,

Lorraine

November 3, 1995

Dear Susan,

I had to write to tell you that your performance these last few days has been nothing short of extraordinary. You utterly captured the agony of withdrawal and moved us deeply. I know I speak for all the writers, who have called and reported how bowled over they were by what you have done.

My other tiny treat, truly amazing, Susan, is that even without makeup, you still look beautiful. It has truly been a pleasure to write for you. Erica is still the richest, most interesting character in daytime, and you are still playing her to perfection.

Thank you! And Brava!

Love,

Lorraine

I was honored and touched to receive such notes from Lorraine. They remain so very meaningful to me. Knowing I had these women in my corner—and their full support, professionally and emotionally—well, that was more than I could have ever asked for.

I am beyond grateful for such wonderful mentors and role models in my life. For me, role models for women are like guiding lights (no pun intended!). They show us what's possible; they remind us of our own strength. Growing up, I remember looking up to women who defied the odds, who stood tall in the face of adversity and carved paths in places where there were none before. My grandmother, whom I called Nana, was one of these women. She was my mother's mother, and I loved that she was so jolly. She had such a warm spirit. Nana was exactly what a grandmother should be: kind, loving, supportive, and solid.

Nana, my only American grandparent, was the first one up in the morning and the last to go to bed at night. She loved to laugh, played the piano for us, cooked delicious meals, and baked the best cakes, pies, and even fresh bread every day. Needless to say, my dad loved her and her cooking. They got along so well. My most vivid memories of Nana revolve around music and food. I know the first time I ever heard Gershwin, Cole Porter, and Irving Berlin was when Nana played them on her piano. I loved spending time in the kitchen with her every day while she made the most wonderful treats. Nana never used a mixer. She beat all of her ingredients by hand. I remember sitting with her while she held her favorite green mixing bowl full of cake batter on her lap, or put the finishing touches on a delicious apple or lemon meringue pie, or made dumplings or donuts or fudge, all of which I loved to eat. She taught me what it meant to be a great cook—something my mother and I never really came around to being ourselves, but we greatly appreciated those who were. (One of the many things I loved about Helmut!)

When we weren't spending time together in the kitchen, Nana sat patiently in her favorite chair and let me create many hairdos for her, with her fox terrier, Snookie, lying by her side. I would set part of her hair in pin curls and part of it in rollers. She had sandy-colored hair laced with gray. She said she had "plaid hair." Nana never cared how it turned out, as long as we were having fun together, which, of course, we were. Since Nana lived with us, my mother never had to cook, and that suited her just fine. My mother definitely preferred to do the cleaning. In fact, she kept a spotless and organized home.

Nana was a very proud and strong woman. I learned later that her husband, my Swedish grandfather, went back to Sweden and wrote her a letter saying he didn't want to be married anymore. Well, my grandmother wouldn't accept any child support or alimony from him. Instead, she was a very good piano player. She started her own orchestra and played piano in the hotels in the Pocono Mountains near the small Swedish German community where she lived. She also accompanied the old silent movies that were shown in their local movie house, as well as the Broadway tryouts that brought their productions to the Milford Opera House, which looked more like a quintessential Andrew Wyeth barn than a classic opera house. I have always been very proud of my grandmother for how she was self-reliant and how she managed to care for her children as a single mother. She was so ahead of her time. She chose to take her talent and do something with it rather than sit around and wallow in her sadness.

Divorce wasn't very common back in those days. I am sure it was a challenge for the whole family because there weren't a lot of single women role models then for my grandmother to look up to or emulate. Hearing these stories as a young girl gave me the eyes to see and the ears to hear so that I could relate to all sorts of situations I would encounter growing up. These weren't my experiences, but they were poignant and important to the person I would later become.

I am so grateful my mother gave me some of my grandmother's jewelry, cookie cutters, and the green crockery mixing bowl Nana used all the time. I also have some sheet music from her days of playing the piano for the Broadway tryouts. I have those framed and hanging in my house. One of those has special meaning for me—the sheet music from the original Broadway production of *Annie Get Your Gun*. It took my breath away when I found it—I played Annie Oakley in the revival of that show on Broadway. I keep it on the wall in my dressing room at my home.

Now, my mother was someone I always turned to for her fashion and design eye and for life advice. She was my go-to. Not just because she was my mother but because I trusted her. She had so many insights that were uniquely hers—and I really valued them. Her directness and honesty were something I could count on, and I loved her for always telling it like it was. As my career took off, my mother also became my eyes, meaning she watched everything I ever did, whether it was *All My Children*, a talk show, QVC—whatever it was. When the show was over, I would always call her and ask her what she thought. It became our ritual. And she always told me as she saw it.

My mother was a very beautiful woman. She had fabulous, naturally red hair, perfect fair skin, and a gorgeous sprinkle of freckles. My mother was very soft-spoken yet not afraid to share her opinions. She had great taste, a real flair for interior design, was full of common sense, and had a stubborn streak.

I remember one summer day, when I was about eleven or twelve, my mother gave me my first copy of *Seventeen* magazine. She said she thought I would enjoy it. The girls on those pages were all beautiful teenagers with such nice hair. I was mesmerized by all the posing and grown-up fashion. I fantasized about becoming like the models I saw in the pages of that magazine. The only problem was, I am very petite, and my hair is dark and naturally curly. I didn't look like a typical or perfect girl. I had spent my youth watching my mother take very good care of her skin and her health, a practice she passed on to me. However, it was *Seventeen* magazine that helped me understand how important all of those things are, especially for a young girl. That was the day I realized there was a whole wide world out there to be discovered, and I wanted to be in it!

During high school, my mother started taking me to New York City to see Broadway shows. She knew I wanted to be an actress and thought I would love to go. We mostly went when I was off from school or during summer vacations. Although New York City was only an hour away from our home, we rarely made the drive into the city. My father thought New York was a very tough place, especially for women to go on their own. Still, my mother and I loved the excitement of planning a special day together to take in the latest play and have lunch at Sardi's, a place we had read about in the newspapers, the most famous eatery in the theater district. As the story goes, the owner of Sardi's, Vincent Sardi, was so good to actors—especially out-of-work actors—he'd offer them the same menu at reduced prices. To this day, it is a well-known hangout for the theater crowd, both actors and patrons.

We spent wonderful days together seeing everyone from Richard Burton in *Hamlet* to Sammy Davis Jr. and Lola Falana in *Golden Boy*. That production of *Hamlet* was very contemporary looking. It was beautiful and spellbinding, and I have never forgotten Richard Burton's presence on the stage. I was fourteen, and it was the first time I ever looked at an older man and thought he was sexy. And Eileen Herlie, who I would end up working with years later on *All My Children*, played his mother, Gertrude. (I was speechless when I met Eileen years later and actually got to work with her. She was so elegant, and she'd had such an illustrious career.)

On the way out of the theater, I somehow got swept up in the sea of people leaving the show. I found myself thrust up against the rear window of a waiting limousine. My mother was trying to rescue me but was unable to reach my hand through the crowd. I was smack up against that window, and I could see Richard Burton sitting in the back seat! He had his arms around two young girls. I don't know why, but I thought one of them might have been Elizabeth Taylor's daughter, Liza Todd. Richard Burton looked so protective of those girls. He saw me peering through the window; he couldn't miss me or my smooshed body against the glass. We gazed at each other for mere seconds, and I was completely mesmerized—he had the bluest eyes! I was absolutely thrilled to have had that moment with Richard Burton, someone who was larger than life.

When my mother took me to see *Golden Boy*, I begged her to let me wait outside the stage door so I could catch a glimpse of Sammy Davis Jr. Even as a teenager, I recognized Sammy Davis as one of the greatest performers of all time, and I wanted to get his autograph. Well, we stood outside that door for hours, but he never came out. As I turned to my mother to say that we could finally leave, Miss Lola Falana was standing right in front of me. I remember watching her on *The Ed Sullivan Show*—and there she was! It was so exciting for me. I still remember she was wearing jeans, an oversized crisp white men's shirt, and sneakers. She was gorgeous. This was the first time I ever saw a dancer in person.

I didn't know what to say. I gasped and said, "You're Lola Falana!" Then I added, "I've seen you on TV and everything!" I sounded like a giddy schoolgirl, which, of course, I was.

She looked at me and didn't say anything. She just turned away and ran down the street. Moments after that exchange, I told myself, "When I grow up and become a famous actress, I am definitely going to sign autographs!" I have never forgotten what it was like to be a wide-eyed girl full of hopes and dreams.

This tradition of taking in Broadway shows and spending time together in the city became something my mother and I did regularly throughout high school and into my college years. I was so lucky because my college roommate, Patty Johnson (née Dupuy), loved theater too, and her mother would take us to see Broadway shows, including some of the most amazing ones! We saw *Funny Girl* with Barbra Streisand, *Hello, Dolly!* with Carol Channing, and *Fiddler on the Roof* with Zero Mostel. Patty and I were the two happiest girls on the planet. Anyone would love to have Patty in the audience, as she was so enthusiastic during every performance. (To this day, Patty and I still see shows together whenever she comes to New York!)

Each of these women taught me that it's okay to be both tender and fierce, to dream boldly, and to be a doer. They showed me that success isn't always about perfection but about determination and authenticity. Their stories intertwined with my own, making me braver, bolder, and more hopeful about what I could achieve.

As my career took off, I'd encounter many other women who would have a lasting impact and impression on my life. Very early in my career, I received a call from Dennis Swanson, who was the president of ABC Daytime for a number of years while I was there. Dennis asked if I would mind doing an interview after work one day. He said that when I finished filming *All My Children*, I could walk across the street to another studio and do the interview with someone he believed in very much. She was from Baltimore and was in New York City for a couple of days. Of course, I agreed. After we wrapped, I went across the street to the studio and met a young reporter named Oprah Winfrey. She was unknown at the time. Dennis was very much in her corner, and after I did the interview, I understood why. The studio had a small audience, which I wasn't expecting. When we finished the interview, I turned to Oprah and said, "You just gave me one of the best interviews I have ever experienced." She asked great questions and then asked follow-up questions. I never once felt like she was just going down a list of prepared notes. That is quite rare, and I really appreciated that she made me feel like she was truly listening, as if we were having a conversation and not just an interview. There is something about Oprah that makes her so relatable. She was so at ease, very warm and inquisitive—in a good way. From the start of her career, I believe Oprah has had a broader appreciation for stories that captivate and connect with audiences emotionally. She has intellectual curiosity and a lovely way about her. I'd later learn that Oprah was a devoted fan of *All My Children*. Yes, Oprah Winfrey! She even described herself as "obsessed" with the show. Apparently, she admired the strong storytelling and compelling characters, particularly Erica Kane. Her affection for the series was so well-known that she once welcomed the cast of *All My Children* onto *The Oprah Winfrey Show* to celebrate the show's legacy. I was one of those guests and always loved talking with her.

Several years ago, I attended a fundraiser in New York for a wonderful organization called Little Flower Children and Family Services of New York. This organization is dedicated to improving the lives of children, families, and individuals with developmental disabilities across the New

York area. Families who are in peril can drop their children off anytime, day or night. Volunteers come on their own dime to hold the babies, to give them love and attention. Ever since my time in the NICU with Andreas, I have tremendous empathy for anyone going through this.

During the first cocktail reception I attended in support of Little Flower Children, I observed the most chic and dynamic woman, Billie Walsh. She was a notable figure with deep roots in New York's cultural and philanthropic communities I was told she was a founding partner of Jimmy Ryan's 52nd Street, a well-known New York City jazz club in the 1940s. I was in awe and completely intrigued. She was very elegant and so impressive. Not in a flashy way. She was simply herself. I wanted to know more about her life.

Billie was married to Thomas L. Walsh for sixty years until his passing. While he was off fighting in World War II, she was busy running the jazz club—talk about cool. She and her husband eventually had two children as well as thirteen grandchildren and twenty-one great-grandchildren!

When I met Billie, I wish I'd had the wherewithal to interview her. She was utterly fascinating and extremely inspiring to me in so many ways. I knew she must have had some incredibly interesting stories and no doubt a great deal of wisdom and advice on life, love, resilience, and surviving. In fact, I remember wishing at that time that I was a producer because I wanted to interview her and the remaining women of the Greatest Generation. To this very day, I regret not getting that together.

Another woman I respected and greatly admired was Marylou Whitney. Marylou always looked beautiful and had the most gorgeous skin. She was very youthful, a generous philanthropist, and full of great adventure. She also had the best Christmas cards! Her cards were a compilation of whatever she was doing over the previous year. In one photo, she'd be on a motorcycle; in another, she'd be playing poker with the guys. If she went salmon fishing, she would catch the salmon, poach it, and then serve it for dinner at her beautifully set table. I have always believed that in life, you should just be you, and she was one of the most original and authentic people I've ever known. She was one phenomenal lady and a wonderful role model for me and all who knew her.

I first met Marylou when we attended a party at her home in Kentucky during the Derby weekend. I remember seeing two very large urns atop the pillars at the front gate. The urns were filled with freshly cut flowers, which had been placed there by hand. When we approached the front door, I was expecting to be greeted by a butler or some other member of her household staff. Much to my surprise, Marylou answered the door herself. She was the most gracious hostess ever. She always greeted every single one of her guests. She looked exquisite, dressed in a beautiful white gown, with a crown of white flowers in her hair. I had the privilege to meet her then-husband, C. V. "Sonny" Whitney, who joined her at the door. Although we had never met, I could see his health was fading. Still, he was every bit as gracious as his wife.

Marylou and I hit it off from the very start and forged a lovely connection that night at her party. A few months later, I was being honored by the Red Cross in Palm Beach. Marylou had a home there and asked if I would attend a party she was hosting the afternoon before the event. Of course, I said I would be delighted. I was seated at her table, between two very charming men. As soon as I sat down, they each leaned over and said, "Welcome to Erica Kane County." We all laughed and had the best time for the rest of the afternoon. At one point, Marylou excused herself from the table so she could mingle with her other guests. I watched as she floated across the room, going from one guest to another, making each feel welcome and like an old friend. I learned so much about what it means to be a great hostess from watching Marylou. After that, Marylou and I developed a very special friendship. She was one of the most delightful and strongest women I've ever known.

Several years after Sonny died, Marylou met John Hendrickson, another wonderful man, whom she married in 1997. John was a former aide to Governor Walter Joseph Hickel of Alaska. He quickly became one of my favorite people to be around. He was such a good guy and very funny. He was always my first choice to be seated next to at a dinner party!

Helmut and I visited Marylou and John many times at their home in Saratoga Springs in upstate New York, where she was known as "The Queen of Saratoga." We attended their annual gala during the height of the horse-racing season. I love Saratoga and the Adirondacks, so I was always happy to spend time in that region, especially with Marylou and John.

In addition to being one of the greatest beauties and legendary hostesses of all time, Marylou was a champion and very hands-on Thoroughbred horse breeder and one of the greatest adventure seekers I have ever met. We were thrilled when she asked if Helmut and I would be interested in taking a trip with her and John to Alaska to experience the Iditarod. The first Iditarod race was held in 1973, with thirty-four dogsled teams passing through twenty-six checkpoints on the route. This is no race for the fainthearted. To be clear, Helmut and I were not manning a dogsled team, but I would be doing a ride-along for the first leg of the race with a professional musher. We were primarily there to be with Marylou. And adding to the fun, we were joined by the legendary Joan Rivers. Each of us would ride individually with a musher for the first eleven miles of the race.

The night before the start of the race, we attended what is known as the Musher's Banquet. I was happy to learn several female mushers were participating in the race that year. One of them came over to me and said, "Wait until you get on the sled and pull out of the city limits. All you will hear is the sound of the dogs' paws on the snow." I thought that sounded fantastic and could hardly wait!

The next morning, the sun was shining, and the sky was a brilliant, bright blue. It was bone-chilling cold too. You couldn't recognize any of us that day because we were so bundled up. However, Marylou somehow managed to look glamorous in those freezing cold conditions. I wore a sweater that my "Norwegian mother" had made for me herself when I was sixteen years old and an exchange student. I was all set to ride along for the first eleven miles of the race. The musher I traveled with gave me a comfortable pillow to sit on because these are very bare-bones sleds. They want to keep things as aerodynamic as they can. He also gave me a stuffed animal husky to hold on to for good luck. My Iditarod experience lasted for a total of forty-five minutes. Unfortunately, it went by in a flash. It was so exciting and fun that I actually forgot how cold it was. People all along the route were cheering for us as we passed and throwing home-baked muffins and even salmon for the musher. Having the opportunity to participate in the Iditarod, even just a little, was an experience I loved and will never forget—one I would have never encountered had it not been for Marylou.

Sadly, Marylou passed away on July 19, 2019. After Helmut passed, John and I spoke fairly regularly. We had lost our loves—our partners in life. It helped having someone to talk to—and as I said, John had a wonderful sense of humor, which I really loved. I was completely shocked when I heard that John died suddenly on August 19, 2024. Losing both of these friends was hard, yet I remain so grateful for the incredible impact they had on me and their friendship, which I will always cherish. Marylou was, and remains, a great inspiration to me and all who knew her.

I think there is so much value in storytelling, especially as we've become a disconnected society. I just love when the generations come together. There is so much wisdom that the Greatest Generation and boomers have to impart—and I have always been a willing and eager learner. I also believe that we have so much to learn from the generations coming up behind us too. I think they have such interesting things to say. I admire the people who help us rise above and who appeal to our hearts instead of just to a specific religion or political party. These individuals speak to our humanity. They touch us and offer us hope and inspiration.

Chapter Seven:

AGING WITH AUDACITY

Don't try to "age with grace." Age with mischief, audacity, and a good story to tell.

—AUTHOR UNKNOWN

I've never loved the notion of growing old gracefully. No, you can bet I am going kicking and screaming, that's for sure. I've heard it said that the key to aging well is laughter, friends, and a really good moisturizer. Yes, I think this is true. And sunblock too.

When I was twenty-eight years old, I caught sight of myself in the rearview mirror of my car. I was not wearing sunglasses at the time. It was a warm and sunny summer day. I noticed I was squinting. In that moment, I thought, *I should probably start wearing sunglasses, and probably start using a little moisturizer around my eyes.* If I kept squinting, I thought I might get lines around my eyes, and I wasn't ready for that. Call it an aha moment or call it vanity, this was how I felt. Besides, my mother, who had the most gorgeous skin, had set the bar pretty high when it came to aging. She was the best role model and certainly passed along many of her beauty secrets and her joie de vivre. Even then, I knew my mom was full of spunk. She cut her own hair, never had it colored. She was a natural redhead. She used Clinique moisturizer when she had it. She definitely was not high maintenance. And she had such a passion for life. I think this was her best beauty tip of all.

I turned sixty and became a grandmother on the same day. The reality was great. But the new label took some getting used to. Not long before this milestone birthday, I had read that once you turn sixty, people look at you and think, *Wow. Now you're old.*

I will admit, I didn't feel old. I didn't even think I looked old, but there I was, sixty and now a grandmother.

I called my mother, who was now ninety years old and who always told it like it was, and I asked her, "Mom, how did you do it? How did you deal with turning sixty?"

She listened carefully. There was a slight pause, and then she said, "Well, I just don't think about it."

I thought that was great advice.

Besides, we aren't mind readers.

Who can say what other people really think when they see us?

And if they are judging us, does it really matter?

As long as you're doing what you love and not being your own worst enemy, there is no need to put any of that pressure on yourself, thinking, *Now I am old. Now I am _____ (fill in the blank).* Don't let your age define you because it doesn't define you.

For years, I loved reading Oprah Winfrey's magazine, *O*. I would always take it on airplanes with me, reading it from cover to cover. I think I made Helmut crazy, nudging him with my elbow and sharing one brilliant article after the next. I was always learning something new from reading that magazine. Many times, Oprah shared her reflections on aging, particularly the wisdom and self-assurance that come with entering a new decade. I remember when she turned fifty, she shared some advice that her mentor, Maya Angelou, gave her. She said, "Babe, the fifties are everything you've been meaning to be."[1] Another reason to love Maya Angelou.

And I admired Oprah too, especially when I heard her say that she had gained wisdom in her fifties. But when I think about my fifties, I didn't really feel like my wisdom had kicked in yet. *Maybe,* I wondered, *now that I've turned sixty, will that "wisdom" Oprah talked about finally come to me with this new decade?* Believe me, I was in no hurry to grow older, but I craved the wisdom that comes with experience, and slowly, in my sixties, I did feel that wisdom starting to creep in.

Not everybody is built alike. I saw my mother take good care of herself, and that inspired me to follow her example. I really believe in taking it one day at a time. If you take good care of yourself and you're in great shape today, you're going to look good and be in great shape tomorrow. I also believe that it is easier to take care of yourself day by day instead of letting things get away from you and feeling overwhelmed.

Feeding the soul is extremely important to me. Gratitude feeds my soul. My relationship with God certainly feeds my soul. As does my relationship with the Blessed Mother, Mary. While my mother was not an overtly religious woman, one thing she did pass on to me was a devotion to the Blessed Mother. A lot of Catholic girls were instilled with this belief, and it is the truth for me. It's also very personal.

When my mother was in her nineties and still living alone, I would call her, and she would be standing on the dining room table, shining the crystals in the chandelier. While I appreciated her independence and determination, I also knew this was probably quite dangerous for her, especially at her age. But that was my mom—she wasn't about to give up any of her independence. Like me, she faced aging kicking and screaming. The apple doesn't fall far from the tree.

However, she was becoming more stubborn than ever. Her hearing loss was increasing, and she was refusing to wear hearing aids. She said, "No, Susan, people will think I am old." My mother never wanted anyone to think she was old. Ever.

When I'd speak to her on the phone, I found myself nearly shouting so she could hear me.

"Mom, Mom . . ."

She'd say, "Susan, I can't hear you—I have the phone to my bad ear."

"Mom, put the phone to your good ear!" I'd say even louder.

Of course, I had to laugh. If she couldn't hear me in her bad ear, how would she move the phone to her good ear? I remember thinking, *This should be a scene in a movie.* Okay, well, at least a scene in my book.

Even though my mother had fallen and broken the same hip twice, she insisted on wearing her leopard-print kitten heels with the walker.

It wasn't until several years later that her trusted nurse finally convinced her to wear flats or black sneakers, something I had never seen my mother wear before. At one point, Helmut tried to buy her a better walker with wheels instead of the one she was using with bright yellow tennis balls on the ends. He explained to her that she was a beautiful woman, who was very fashionable. A new walker would allow her to stand up straighter, and she could feel more like herself. It even had a basket she could place her heavy purse in. Mom always carried a purse, and you can bet that bag was never leaving her arm, even while using her walker. Despite Helmut's best efforts, my mother was not having any of it. In fact, on the day Helmut brought my mother to check out new walkers, she took one look at the model he had in mind, and she threw it clear across the store.

I remember calling her once at her house in Palm Beach when she was still living alone. It was Fourth of July weekend. When she answered, I asked, "Mom, how are you doing?"

"Well, I was reading the newspaper this morning, and I saw that Lowe's is having a sale on red bricks. So, I went down there, and I bought the red bricks. I've always wanted to fill in the terra-cotta patio where the plants, shrubbery, and flowers are. I just always thought there was a place there that needed a little finishing."

Somebody helped her to the car; however, she loaded the bricks into the trunk, got to her house, unloaded them two at a time, and brought them to her patio. She was determined to fill in that gap! And sure enough, those bricks were lined up perfectly, putting the finishing touch on her patio, just the way she'd imagined it would!

I never wanted to be the daughter who dragged her mother kicking and screaming out of her house, insisting she needed to be somewhere I could be sure she was safe and well cared for. I always thought I would do it only if it were medically indicated, if her doctors concurred and told me it was time. If you've dealt with an aging parent, I'm sure you can understand this dilemma. Not long after the bricks incident, I realized my mother was having some problems with knowing the time of day. She was experiencing a little cognitive decline. That's when I knew it was time to move her into an assisted-living environment.

The first place she tried out was more of an independent-living facility because she qualified for that. They had five dining rooms. The men shaved and showered and wore sport coats to dinner. It appeared there were some interesting people there, and my mom, at ninety-eight, looked beautiful. Yes, even at ninety-eight.

"Mom, you're going to be the belle of the ball. I think you're going to love it there," I told her.

I was wrong.

She didn't love it. She didn't even like it. She wasn't ready to leave her home.

I understood how she felt, so I moved her back into her house and found some help she wouldn't fire, so she would be properly cared for.

Even so, my mother fired everyone we hired to help her. Everyone, that is, except for Mary Pennington, who was her best friend's daughter. Mary was a very accomplished nurse and the head of nursing at the independent-living facility my mother had just come from.

Within the year, perhaps six months later, I started getting calls from Mary that my mother had fallen again a number of times. Three different doctors examined her, asking her simple questions, such as "Do you know where you are?" referring to the hospital she was in.

"Don't ask me any trick questions. I'm not an architect!" my mother responded very matter-of-factly.

"What year is it?" and "Do you know who the president is?"

Sadly, my mother was unable to answer correctly.

I also started to notice that she had been sleeping a lot more. I would occasionally call her midday, and she would already be in bed for the night. Then she'd get up in the evening, turn on the lights, and think it was daytime. She didn't know day from night.

I am so grateful that my mother never got ornery, which can often happen when someone slips into a state of dementia. She remained soft-spoken and was able to make herself known and express her preferences. She was never emotionally out of control. She always recognized Helmut and me when we came to visit, but I also began to notice things she was no longer able to recognize.

One of my mother's favorite shows was *The Voice*. She enjoyed the music, but I think the real reason she watched was because she thought Blake Shelton was very handsome. I'd call her every Monday, the night the show aired, to remind her to watch. When she didn't recognize the name of the show, I would say, "You know, Mom. The one with Blake Shelton, the very handsome guy from Oklahoma who sings."

"Oh, yes." That description prompted recognition, if only for a moment.

As hard as it was for me to acknowledge, she was in the beginning stages of dementia. That's when the doctors recommended that she go to assisted living.

When she was first diagnosed, it took me a while to grasp what was happening. I was upset because I was never sure if she had dementia or if she just couldn't understand what was being said due to her hearing loss. As her dementia progressed, it was very hard for me to accept that my mother was not the mother I knew. She was no longer totally accessible.

My mother and I were very close. She was my biggest cheerleader. And yet she talked very straight to me, which I loved, *always*. From the time I was a little girl, she didn't sugarcoat anything. When I was fourteen years old, I competed in a local tennis tournament in a neighboring community. During one of my matches, my mother was sitting in the stands to watch me play. It was a hot, humid summer day. I thought I played pretty well, but I didn't win. When I saw her afterward, she turned to me and said, "You looked like rigor mortis set in." She thought I should have chased down the ball more and run faster if I were going to become competitive. When I was in college, while the other girls' mothers were telling them to eat something, my mother was saying, "Watch your hips, honey." She didn't mean any harm by saying things like this to me. It was her "country wisdom," and I think there is a certain pragmatism in that. My mother was an RN, an OR nurse, and a member of the Greatest Generation, which meant she had to be a realist—she had to be practical. These were good lessons and good things for me to know. And by the way, I did get better at tennis after that.

Like most mothers and daughters, my mom and I didn't always see eye to eye, but we loved each other immensely—unconditionally—as only a mother can love their child, and vice versa. Many years before she passed, there was a period of a few months when I was not talking to my mother. I was really angry with her, but I continued to love her. Always. And we made up. Always.

As time went by, I realized we were brought up in different ways. After all, my mother was raised during the Great Depression by a single mom. Her father left when she was five years old. I wasn't raised like that. I had a completely different childhood. Now with hindsight, I realize my mother had a very different life experience than I did. So, of course, we were going to come from a different place regarding how we experienced certain things. Once I understood this, any animosity I had simply melted away. I think true unconditional love exists, especially from the mother to the child. It doesn't always come back the other way, but I do believe that it exists.

For my mother's one hundredth birthday, Helmut and I hosted a party at her favorite restaurant in Palm Beach, Café L'Europe. I would take her there after she lost my dad, and she always loved it. There used to be a jazz combo that would play on Thursday, Friday, and Saturday nights. My mother loved jazz, and she would sway to the music. The drummer must have noticed her passion for the music because one time, just as we were leaving, he handed her his drum brushes and asked her to sit down and play a set with them. And she did! My mother wasn't a performer, but she was always authentically herself. She once told me that as a little girl, she used to lie in her bed and dream of being a big band singer, but as far as I know, she never pursued that dream. Her life would have taken her down a very different path.

Not long ago, a friend asked if I am my own worst critic. I was a little taken aback by the question, and I had to think about it for a moment. Then I said, "I hope so."

Here's what I mean.

I hope there is no one out there who could possibly be harder or more critical of me than I am on myself. That would be really hard to accept, although it usually motivates me, as in the examples of tennis and, of course, losing the Emmy. While there is an initial sting in the truth, it always makes me want to take it to heart and do better. Even my mother's keen observations were no match for my own self-assessments. And yet, when you think about it, why are we, especially women, so hard on ourselves in the first place? Why can't we exhibit unconditional love for ourselves as we do for our loved ones? How do you give unconditional love to someone else if you can't give it to yourself? I know I live with a strong moral compass and have certain standards for myself. I would be deeply ashamed if I did certain things that were in conflict with those standards. I think it's an interesting question. What I know is that you can be self-critical and still love yourself. They're not mutually exclusive.

I think acceptance and self-love are journeys that begin within ourselves. Embracing ourselves means acknowledging our flaws while celebrating our unique strengths. Self-love isn't about perfection; it's about recognizing our inherent worth despite life's challenges. In the words of RuPaul, "If you can't love yourself, how in the hell are you gonna love somebody else?"

My mother's nurse, Mary, would often use the word *acceptance* with me. This was a word I had given very little thought to before my mother's health began to decline. Mary explained that there are some things you cannot change. Even if it is in your nature to always try to accomplish what you want to do or what you think is best, you will sometimes come up against that which you cannot change. This was a difficult but wonderful lesson for me to learn in many ways, and it would take time to fully understand and embrace it.

For six years, I watched my mother go through different phases of deterioration, and still she always found a way to make herself understood. She was her usual self in many ways, and yet, she wasn't the same. And for the last four years of her life, I no longer had my mother as I had always known her. This was a completely different type of loss than I had ever experienced. Losing someone you love, yet knowing they are still alive. Well, this was hard to bear and certainly a challenge to accept.

My mother was born in 1917 amid the Spanish flu pandemic and experienced global-changing events, from two world wars and the Great Depression, all the way through the birth of the internet, and then COVID. I wasn't able to be with my mother for nearly a year because of COVID. I called and spoke to her all the time, but I didn't see her in person again until February 2021. For a year I asked the nursing staff, "Please, if you see my mother taking a turn for the worse, please call me so I can get on the next plane from New York. I don't want my mother to die alone."

By May, I received that dreaded call. My mother had suddenly taken a turn toward the end of life—I only hoped and prayed I would get to her in time. I am eternally grateful to God and her wonderful hospice nurses that I did. I was there with her. I was able to tell her all the good things about her, how much I loved her, how proud I had always been of her—and hopefully I was able to bring her peace.

By now you know how spunky my mom was—I'm sure that determination really helped her to reach 104 years old! My mom was a survivor and thriver, and I am so thankful to God, despite whatever differences we might have had, that she was my mom.

I want to share something that Cathy Thibedeau (née Gasperina), another good friend from college who knew my mom since our college days, wrote to me when my mom passed away:

"Our mothers live on in us, with buoyant spirit!"

Oh, YES! I couldn't agree more.

I miss my mother very much. And yet, I have so much gratitude for the years we had together—for the unbreakable bond and the unconditional love we shared.

Chapter Eight:

UNFORGETTABLE

Being unforgettable means having an absence
that is felt just as much as your presence.
—C. JOYBELL C.

Helmut was raised in Austria by a single mother. One of his earliest childhood memories was rushing to the bomb shelter in Innsbruck. He was two years old, and when his mother heard the sirens, she would take him by the hand while holding his baby brother, Gunther, in her arms and rush them to safety.

As the war waged on, Helmut's mother heard of a woman named Lena who was taking in young children to keep them safe from the bombings. In an effort to protect her children, she took Helmut and Gunther to live with this woman in the Austrian Alps, not far from Innsbruck, where they were born. The Alm, where they stayed, was very high up in the mountains, nearly above the tree line. An Alm is a large pasture where the farmers move their cows in the summertime because it's much cooler up there. Helmut's mom knew this would be a safe location, even if it meant she would not be with them. Helmut and Gunther lived with their "foster mother," Lena, for nearly six years, until the end of the war. Their mother came to visit them every Sunday, riding her bike for two hours to the base of the mountain and then walking with her bike for two hours more to the top of the mountain. That's where Lena's farmhouse was—where she was taking in children from the city below to keep them safe from the bombing.

Helmut and I traveled to Austria often to visit his family. During one trip we took around 2005, Helmut and I were driving in the mountains when he casually pointed and said, "Do you see that village way up there? That's where I was with Lena. Would you want to drive up there and see it?"

"Yes, of course!" I was so excited.

Helmut had told me about Lena, so I was excited he was taking me to see where he spent much of his early childhood. If you've never been to one of these Austrian mountain villages, it's hard to imagine how beautiful they are. It's also hard to imagine how people built their houses there—some hanging off the edge of the majestic mountain at an altitude so high that almost no trees grow. On the way, Helmut turned to me and said, "I don't think anyone up here has ever seen an American." It's not like there was the internet or television, so even though this was many years after the end of the war, I thought he might be right—and I was so curious.

We drove up and up and up this winding mountain road until we came to a plateau. It was very open with only dirt roads and a farmhouse, where we came across several little boys playing cops and robbers, cowboys and Indians. Now, this was many years after Helmut had been there, and we were both surprised to see the young boys playing the same games Helmut had played, climbing those same trees. Helmut pulled the car over to the side of the road. As we got out, he pointed toward the farmhouse and said, "This is it. This is the house I lived in as a little boy during the war."

Way down the dirt road, we could see an older woman dressed in all black walking toward us. As she came closer, we noticed she was carrying a bag. She had been to the local bakery for fresh bread, as is the daily custom there. As she got closer to us, I noticed some of her teeth were missing. She was quite elderly and had lived in the mountains her whole life. Her cheeks were rosy and her eyes so bright, I marveled at her. Every line on her face told a story. Helmut and I didn't speak as she made her way toward us.

"Helmut?" she asked.

I couldn't believe it. Helmut and I were stunned.

It was Lena—and she remembered him after all this time!

Decades had passed since they had seen one another, and Helmut had been a little boy when they said their last goodbye. And yet, she recognized him as if they had seen each other yesterday. Helmut always had a certain presence—a way of standing, a big personality, full of *gemütlichkeit*, a German word that refers to the joy of living, friendliness, and good cheer.

But even so, for Lena to remember him and call him by name without any hesitation! *That* was amazing.

Being there and running into Lena defied my expectations as we made our way to the farmhouse that day. Lena and my husband had a wonderful and unexpected reunion that is hard to put into words. Although Lena didn't speak any English, she was so kind and warm toward me. My German is very limited, but I managed to let her know how grateful I was to meet her. We had a lovely exchange before Lena invited us to come inside her home because, of course, she wanted to feed us. Naturally, we went in and sat at her kitchen table—a simple traditional Austrian wooden table—while she sliced the freshly baked bread she'd just bought. And then she did something I'd never seen. She climbed up a ladder into her chimney and took down a side of bacon that she had been smoking. Helmut told me that once it is smoked like that, it is safe to eat just as it is and quite delicious!

We sat with Lena at her farm table while she and Helmut reminisced about their time together all those years ago. It was a spectacular experience for both Helmut and me.

He shared that when his mother visited, she would be the one to give the boys a bath.

"We were wild boys, off playing in our lederhosen, which could stand up all by themselves by the end of the week. We had dirt embedded in our heels!" Helmut said before letting out one of his contagious laughs. He remembered how his mother would scrub their heels with a brush to get them clean. He spent an hour or more telling me what it had been like, talking about why his mother had put him and Gunther there. He understood that she wanted to keep them safe. During our visit with Lena, Helmut shared his memories of seeing the flashing lights off in the distance from the bombings in nearby cities when he was six. Of course, from high up in the Alps, you could see for many miles, so he and his brother would walk to the edge of the mountain and look over to see the red-and-amber exploding lights of the bombs. At the time, they were completely unaware of what they were looking at. To them, it was just a light show in the valley below.

Listening to Helmut that afternoon, I fell even more in love with him—as if that was even a possibility. But it was. And I did. There was an intimacy in seeing this time in his life I hadn't expected. But I could understand completely how these experiences shaped him into the strong, confident man, son, brother, husband, father, and grandfather he was. Everything he endured during those years gave him an extraordinary strength, wisdom, perspective, and resilience that he was able to tap into as he navigated his later life.

Once Helmut and Gunther returned home to their mother, she did whatever was necessary to make sure her boys were well cared for. Helmut and his brother returned to school and tried to get on with their lives as if the past five or so years had never happened. But they did. Sometimes, Helmut would come home to find a piece of furniture missing.

He'd ask his mother what had happened to the armoire or the table.

"Oh, I have it out being refinished," she'd say.

But that wasn't true. She was selling their furniture to the local farmer so she could get food for them to eat. Of course, Helmut didn't realize it at the time, but he eventually figured it out. Food was so scarce. If Helmut asked his mom to bake a cake, she'd agree only if there was a trade-off—usually, Helmut knitting a pair of socks for himself or his brother.

When I was younger, I often wondered how the women of my mother's generation, especially European women who had been through the war as adults, could be so jolly. They laughed and always looked beautiful in my eyes. I would think, *How can they have this lightness about them when I know what they have seen?* It wasn't until I was older, and after hearing these stories that Lena and Helmut shared with me, that I finally understood it was very likely *because* of what they had seen and survived. This is life.

I had never pushed Helmut to talk about those early years in his life during World War II. But every once in a while, he would tell me about it, and I would listen and try to imagine. Helmut told me a story that I love about how great the American soldiers were to them as children. As little boys, they had little or no food. Helmut and his brother were two of the children who received food in care packages via the Marshall Plan. Sometimes when the American Army jeeps rolled through their town, the soldiers would give Helmut and Gunther chocolates. This was a real high spot in their lives after the war. They were so grateful to the American soldiers.

On the drive back that night, I thought about the first time Helmut took me to the Spanish Riding School in Vienna. Founded in the sixteenth century, the school traces its origins to the Austrian empire's need of well-trained horses for both battle and ceremonial purposes. It is located in the Hofburg palace (also known as the winter palace), in the stunning Baroque Winter Riding Hall, built in 1735.

This world-famous institution is dedicated to the training and performance of Lipizzaner horses, a Spanish breed known for its elegance and grace. The school is renowned for its classical dressage, a highly skilled form of horse training and riding that emphasizes harmony between the horse and its rider. The school hosts events that showcase classical dressage, and executed with exquisite precision. It is a symbol of Austrian culture and an enduring testament to the art of horsemanship.

Guests watch from the gallery above, which wraps around the circumference of the building, as the horses come out to parade—their performances set to classical music. The ground is covered in dirt, yet the horses look exquisite. Above the arena floor, beautiful oil paintings hang along the perimeter walls. It is quite a beautiful experience to have on a Sunday afternoon in Vienna.

As we were leaving, we stepped outside and out of the corner of my eye, I saw a plaque thanking General George Patton and Major General Mark W. Clark, two famous American officers honored for their role in saving the Spanish Riding School during World War II.

"Honey, why are they thanking these American generals?" I asked

Helmut explained that the American military did not bomb the cultural center of the city of Vienna during the war. They only bombed targets that would affect the military. They went out of their way to leave the culture of the city, its treasured iconic buildings, and its heritage in place. As a show of their gratitude for this, the riding school honored these military leaders. Hearing this, I felt a deep sense of pride, both as an American and as the wife of an Austrian who has always cherished America as I do. War is ugly. There's no doubt about that. Still, our American military spared these treasures of Vienna, an act of generosity and kindness that I felt so very grateful for.

I would go anywhere with Helmut, but the many experiences I shared with him in Austria are some of the times I treasure most. I think it is so important to spend time together in your relationship. Helmut once told me early in our marriage that someday we'd have kids and then they'd grow up and we'd be alone together again. I didn't understand what that meant until our kids left home, and it was just the two of us once more. We made it a point to carve out time together as a couple. It is, perhaps, this time, this precious alone time—time I never once took for granted—that I miss the most.

Chapter Nine:

FROM THE HEART

The heart is one of the strongest muscles we have—and the most fragile.

—SONYA TECLAI

While Helmut was a classically trained European chef who loved to cook for me and for our friends when we had them over, we also enjoyed going out for dinner. In October 2018, we were waiting to be seated at one of our favorite places. The maître d' had our waiter walk us to our table when it was ready. As I made my way through the restaurant, I felt a slight pressure on my chest. It was very slight. Like most women, I thought to myself, *It's nothing. It'll go away.* By the time we got to the table, it had, so I didn't give it a second thought.

At the time, my mother was one hundred years old, and I had never had a health issue. My grandmother had passed away of a heart attack and so had my dad, but they each had smoked. Dad preferred Luckys, which were unfiltered cigarettes. My grandmother was a little overweight, mostly from her love of butter, which she cooked and baked with every day. (Can't really blame her for that!) Even with that family history, everyone thought I had my mother's genes, something that always made me happy to think of, so I had no reason to believe otherwise.

A couple of weeks later, we were in another restaurant when the same thing happened. As we were being shown to our table, I felt mild pressure on my chest. Only, this time, it was also radiating around my rib cage to my back. I had never felt anything like that before. I started justifying it to myself with thoughts like, *Maybe I have a new bra on and it's too tight.* Naturally, I knew I didn't, but what else could it be? When I got home that evening, I even checked to see if I was, in fact, wearing a new bra. I wasn't.

A week later, I was in a boutique shopping for a birthday present for a very good friend of mine. The saleswoman stepped aside to wrap it when I felt something I could no longer ignore. In that moment, I remembered seeing a woman being interviewed on TV many years before who had had a heart attack. She wasn't famous, but her story was so powerful, I had never forgotten it. She had talked about how the symptoms for a woman having a heart attack are different from a man's, and what she'd described as her experience was what I was feeling in that moment. It felt like there was an elephant pressing on my chest.

I could not disregard this.

There was a small bench in the boutique near where I was standing. I sat down, and the manager of the boutique, Judi Marti, whom I've known for a long time, came up behind me and said, "Susan, are you all right?"

"Judi, I'm actually sitting here just trying to assess what it is I'm feeling. I am not sure."

"What are you feeling?" she asked.

I told her about the elephant pressing on my chest, and as I spoke, I could see her expression change. While she remained incredibly calm, she said, "Susan, my car is outside. Why don't I drive you to St. Francis? I can get you there faster than an ambulance can arrive." St. Francis Hospital is one of the leading heart hospitals in the country and was about a mile away from the store.

I got into her car, and while we were driving to the hospital, I kept thinking, *This is nothing. It will go away.* Besides, it was my day off. I didn't have time for this. I had so much to do! And I did. I had earmarked that day to run errands and catch up on all the things I had been putting off.

The one thing I didn't have on my to-do list that day?

Taking care of me!

As we were driving to the hospital, it occurred to me that I didn't have a cardiologist. I had no reason to have one, but my husband did. So I called his doctor, Dr. Richard Shlofmitz. I had his private cell phone number, and I knew he had a reputation for always picking up his calls, yet I didn't want to bother him. When he did pick up, I told him I was on my way to the hospital, and then I described my pain.

"Come to the ER. I will meet you there. Your symptoms sound substantial," he said.

I called Helmut to tell him what was happening. All the while, I kept thinking this would go away. I said, "I'm sure this is nothing, but I've called Dr. Shlofmitz, and he wants to see me, so I'm on my way to St. Francis."

No sooner had I spoken those words than Helmut said he was on his way to meet me. I paused for a moment. You see, Helmut had promised our dear friend Nelson DeMille's son James, whose thirteenth birthday was that day, that he would pick him up from school in his Ferrari. James loved cars, and Helmut loved to drive. He was so thrilled that Uncle Helmut was going to pick him up and take him for a drive. We didn't want to disappoint him, and at the time, I really thought I'd be home in an hour or two. So I said, "Please go and pick up James at school." We both agreed it was the right thing to do. In the meantime, my longtime assistant Helene, whom Helmut and I referred to as "Mission Control," came to stay with me until Helmut could arrive.

When Judi and I pulled up to the emergency room, Dr. Shlofmitz was right there. While I was filling out the paperwork, he called my primary care physician, Dr. Holly Andersen. She is also a highly regarded cardiologist at Weill Cornell in New York City, though at that time I never saw her in that capacity. I had only just had a checkup with her a couple of months before, in July. As part of that checkup, I'd even had an EKG, and everything was fine. The doctors at the hospital gave me another EKG that day so they could compare.

Dr. Shlofmitz ordered a CT scan as well. By this time, Helmut had arrived. When the results came back, much to the surprise of us all, the doctor said the test showed I had a 90 percent blockage in my main artery and a 75 percent blockage in the adjacent artery.

I was stunned—I mean absolutely gobsmacked by this revelation.

How could this be?

I'd never had a problem with cholesterol.

I ate salmon, kale, avocado, blueberries—a clean, healthy Mediterranean diet. I worked out almost every day. From the outside, I was the picture of health.

Dr. Shlofmitz, who is a world-renowned cardiologist, turned to me and said, "I can fix this. We can take you right upstairs, and I can put in two stents."

For those of you who may not know, putting in a stent refers to inserting a small tube into a blood vessel, artery, or other passageway to keep it open. This is often done to restore proper blood flow, especially when a vessel has been narrowed or blocked.

In that moment, I had no idea what the doctor was saying to me, but I knew it was serious. It was late, around nine at night, when the results came back.

"We can do the procedure tonight or you can come back first thing in the morning. We can make you first up at six thirty."

The morning sounded better to me. A lot better. Not as urgent, and certainly not as frightening as going into surgery right then and there.

"I'm thinking the morning is good. Your A team will be on their way, and they'll be fresh and ready to go," I said.

"Susan, my A team is already on their way in." The doctor looked quite serious.

"Shouldn't I go home and get a good night's sleep in my own bed and come back and be first up tomorrow morning?" I wasn't stalling. I really thought this might be the best choice.

"I don't think you understand what is happening. You could have a heart attack at any time. It's better to do the surgery now."

That thought had never crossed my mind. *Never.* Not even that day. I was very surprised by the urgency, as was Helmut, who had been diagnosed with A-fib (atrial fibrillation), a common type of irregular heart rhythm, many years prior to my incident.

Helmut had never had a symptom, so he was as surprised as anybody to learn that he had this condition. If you do get this diagnosis, though, you are five times more likely to have a stroke. And if you do have a stroke, you are twice as likely to die from it. So, we knew this information, but it didn't really affect him in any way. There was no lightheadedness, no dizziness, no shortness of breath, nothing. He had to take a blood thinner every day, but other than that, for thirty-plus years after his diagnosis, he lived a very full and fabulous life. We hardly thought about it. And if we did, it was all about Helmut—not me. Dr. Shlofmitz said to me, "You don't look like a heart patient. You can appear healthy, live a healthy lifestyle, eat healthy foods, and still face a life-and-death circumstance with your heart."

Dr. Shlofmitz was rather firm and convincing.

Before I knew what was happening, I was heading up to the operating room, where he had another heart surgeon waiting, just in case they saw more once they were in.

Thankfully, the procedure went well. They placed two stents in, and I was discharged by noon the next day.

I had no pain whatsoever.

By going to the hospital right away and getting the surgery, I *avoided* having a heart attack. I did not *have* a heart attack, but it was a wake-up call, and I became very aware that I would need to stay vigilant with my heart health.

I was so grateful to Dr. Shlofmitz and the nursing staff at St. Francis. Once again, I found myself in the very best hands. Before leaving the hospital, I asked my doctor what he believed caused my blockage. Like my father, the blockage in my arteries turned out to be calcium deposits and not cholesterol. This condition was already in my DNA.

"Susan, one more thing. Don't be alarmed. You will feel a pea-sized nodule by your groin from the procedure. That's just collagen, and it will eventually dissolve."

I said, "Collagen? Really? From the inside? This is good! Can I push it up to my face?"

We both had a good laugh about that.

When my otherwise fabulous dad was in his late forties, he had a mild heart attack. Although I was in my teens, I remember it very well. He was a smoker his whole life. As I said, Luckys with *no filter* were his cigarette of choice. He recovered, but the doctors gave him strict orders to stop smoking. He didn't. My mother, as a former nurse, was on his case about breaking the habit, but that didn't stop him. He cut way back, but he did continue smoking. And sadly, he did end up paying the price later in life.

By the time my father had his second heart attack in 2002, my parents had retired and were living in Florida. My immediate instinct was to bring him to New York. But neither of my parents wanted that. He was very happy with his doctor, who had trained in New York, and he had the utmost confidence in him. The doctors also discovered my father had a large tumor in the upper part of his lung, so he was battling cancer and heart disease at the same time. Unfortunately, my dad did not win that battle. My mother was at the hospital all the time. She jumped right into nursing mode, taking such good care of him. But he didn't make it. The damage to his heart and lungs was too much for him to endure. He passed away in early November of that same year.

As for me, I wasn't a smoker. I ate healthily and was in very good physical shape. There was nothing I could have done to prevent my heart disease. Even so, I asked Dr. Shlofmitz if there was something different I could or should be doing.

"I don't want you to change a thing. I know how you eat. I know you work out almost every day. You don't smoke, and aside from an occasional glass of champagne, you're not drinking." He continued, "Susan, this is really in your DNA. It takes years for calcium to build up." It was something I had inherited from my wonderful dad.

The truth is, I don't think I ever shared my family history with any of my doctors. That was a mistake on my part. I learned that it is extremely important to share your family history from *both* sides with your doctor!

As I was leaving the hospital, the nurse discharging me shared how good it was that I had listened to my body and come in. The nurse told me that I would most likely have had a heart attack and not woken up. The type of blockage I had is commonly referred to as the "widow-maker." I am certain if I had been at home that afternoon instead of out in public, I would have lain down for a bit. Maybe I would have had a sip of water and waited to see how I felt. I can honestly say I don't think I would have gone to the hospital that day if I had been home. And that could have been a game changer for me—as in *game over.*

I was incredibly lucky that I was in that boutique that day; that Dr. Shlofmitz answered his phone; that one of the finest heart hospitals in the country was one mile away; and that Judi, the boutique manager, also had a degree in nursing. What are the odds? I have no doubt that I had a guardian angel on each shoulder that day—my dad on one and my grandmother on the other.

After I was released, Helmut drove me home. First, I was so grateful to be alive. And then, one of my strongest thoughts was to call my publicist, Jessica Sciacchitano, to ask her to help me get this message out. I was lucky enough to have heard that woman's heart attack story all those years ago. I truly believe her story saved my life. Maybe, I thought, by sharing my story now, in real time, if just one woman like me heard it and remembered it, perhaps it could save her life. I felt magnetized, *compelled* to pass my good luck on! The biggest takeaway I wanted to shout from the highest mountain top is this: "Listen to your body! If it's not behaving in a normal way for you, act on it. Don't say, as I did, 'It will go away. It's nothing. I can't disturb this wonderful doctor or take him away from his patients who really need him. I can't _____, I can't _____, I can't _____ (fill in the blanks).'"

And most importantly, put yourself on your to-do list!

Like most women, we take care of our children and loved ones, our life partners and our homes and our careers, and we are nowhere to be found on our to-do list. Even if we are on that list, most of the time, we find our name somewhere at the very bottom. Put yourself on that to-do list. Give yourself permission. Do it for you and the loved ones in your life.

The day I was released, I walked into our kitchen and Andreas was standing there. He said, "Mom, I just had to see for myself that you were okay."

I melted from his being there. I put my arms around Andreas and assured him that I was okay now.

He said he would stay for a while, which always makes me happy. I went upstairs, got dressed, and came down to the kitchen, where he was sitting.

"What are you doing?" Andreas asked in a surprised tone.

"I'm going to take Chris's present to the Garden City Hotel now, where all of our girlfriends are having lunch to celebrate her birthday." I was so nonchalant, going right back to life as usual.

"Mom! Are you crazy? Go put your robe on and stay here. Nobody is going to fault you for missing a birthday luncheon today!" Andreas was adamant.

Helmut overheard our conversation and intervened. "I will take the present to Chris. You stay here."

In the meantime, my publicist, Jessica, did what she does so well, and a few days later, I was on *World News Tonight*, *Today*, and *Good Morning America* and featured in numerous online and print outlets. My heart story became international news. She also put me in touch with the American Heart Association (AHA), the amazing organization I had done a little work with in the past. I've since become a passionate advocate for heart health, actively supporting the AHA, particularly through their Go Red for Women campaign, which "was launched in 2004 with the goal of raising awareness and fighting a woman's greatest health threat—cardiovascular disease. Today, Go Red for Women not only advocates for the health of all women, funds lifesaving research and educates women across the United States and around the world but is committed to removing the unique barriers women face to experiencing better heart health and well-being."[2]

Heart disease is the NUMBER ONE cause of death in women.

More women die from heart disease every year than from all cancers put together.

My passion is to educate women about the importance of recognizing the often subtle symptoms of heart disease. Women tend to experience different symptoms from the classic symptoms experienced by men. In addition, I advocate for regular checkups and heart screenings, including cardiac and carotid artery CT scans, emphasizing the importance of early detection and preventive care. My hope is that my work with the AHA helps spread the message that heart disease is preventable and treatable when addressed early.

As a National Celebrity Ambassador for the AHA's Go Red for Women, I attend their annual event, which takes place at Lincoln Center in New York in February—American Heart Month. There's a red carpet, live entertainment, and a runway for well-known women to walk while wearing red fashions. A few years ago, I was invited to walk the runway in the most gorgeous red gown. It had a big—and I mean *really* big—hoop skirt, which you might think was too much for me to wear, but it wasn't. It was designed beautifully, though it had so many crinolines it was a challenge to move in. In fact, during my final fitting for the gown, Rubin Singer, the designer, was actually under the skirt pinning it to perfection! When it came time for rehearsal, we wore rehearsal clothes—not the actual gown. The people who were in charge of the event kept saying, "Oh, we hope you're going to twirl. We love when you twirl." So when I put the gown on the day of the event, I practiced twirling. No problem.

And then I remembered once, when I was doing *Annie Get Your Gun* on Broadway, I was in the middle of a scene singing "I Got the Sun in the Mornin'," and I was wearing another big satin ball gown (with chunky, heeled cowboy boots) while dancing.

"Got no diamonds. Got no pearls. Still, I think I'm a lucky girl . . ." Anyway, as I went backward, my foot caught my satin dress, and down I went. I popped right up and went on with the show. I didn't think twice about it. That's live theater! Anything can happen. Even so, I didn't want that to happen ever again!

But while I was on the runway for the fashion show in the actual ball gown, I was so excited. The music was playing, and the crowd was so enthusiastic and fabulous. I got to the end of the runway, and playing to the crowd, I spun around just as I had practiced. However, as I twirled to the left, the huge skirt went right, and I caught my heel on its hem, slipped, and fell down.

Splat!

I was shocked. But just like my performance in *Annie Get Your Gun*, I popped up. I had a natural instinct to get back onto my feet. While I was down, I could see a man coming toward me on the stage to help me. Helmut and Andreas were sitting further back than he was, but they were coming to help too, which was so lovely and wonderful. But before any of them got to me, I was on my feet and giving the "okay" sign with my hand. I wanted everyone to know I wasn't hurt, at least not physically. My ego may have been a little bruised, but no big deal.

Chapter Ten:

THE HEART OF THE MATTER

Only when our clever brain and our human heart work together in harmony can we achieve our full potential.

— JANE GOODALL,

Reason for Hope: A Spiritual Journey

Well, you'd think my heart story might have ended there, but it didn't.

Three years later, Helmut was out playing cards with his friends on a Wednesday night, and I was home by myself when I started to feel that pressure in my chest again. I thought, *No, it can't be.* I was in total denial. *No, no. It will go away.*

Mind you, I had just spent the last few years telling people, especially women, to listen to their bodies and not be afraid to call the doctor. And here I was, doing the exact same thing all over again!

When I realized what was happening, I even thought I wasn't going to tell Helmut when he came home. And I didn't. For about half an hour, I kept this discomfort to myself. We went upstairs to go to bed. I took off my makeup as if nothing was wrong. And as I looked at myself in the mirror, I realized I had to tell him.

"You have to call Dr. Shlofmitz. You have to tell him what's happening," he said.

"No, I can't. It's ten thirty. Besides, it's going away. Really. It is." I tried to be convincing, but I am sure Helmut could tell something was wrong.

Okay, even writing this, I can hardly believe I was going there again. But it is what happened. I was being really stubborn.

Then, when I lay down on the bed, I got another symptom—one mostly only women get and one I had not experienced before. It was a sharp pain in my jaw. I had heard of that symptom, but I couldn't understand the connection. So, at first, I thought it might be a toothache. However, when that symptom started coming and going, I knew it was time to call the doctor.

Once again, Dr. Shlofmitz answered right away.

It was a freezing cold January night, and he said he'd meet me at the hospital. This wasn't something he did just for me. This is the kind of doctor he is. This is his reputation.

When I got to the hospital, he did another CT scan. This time, however, both calcium *and* cholesterol were in my arteries. This was the first time cholesterol ever came up for me. And for good reason.

I have a confession.

Forgive me, readers, for I have sinned . . .

So, okay, this happened right after lockdown and the first wave of COVID. I was so grateful for the precious, guilt-free time Helmut and I shared together. It was truly a gift—and I knew it.

He cooked, and I ate.

All the time.

I ate everything that wasn't nailed down. I ate hot Hungarian goulash with warm buttered noodles. I ate bratwurst and mashed potatoes, made even more delicious with lots of butter. And rösti potatoes and spaetzle and pasta and on and on and on . . .You might say I was embracing carb-e diem. Yes, I was seizing the bread! I was rolling in the dough, carb style!

Sure enough, I was loafing around when I should have been saying, "Pasta la vista, baby!"

This was a great departure from my usual diet, and I can't lie, it was fantastic. Helmut made all the comfort foods he grew up eating. I thought of it like it was monopoly food. It wasn't real, because it was COVID.

Can you relate to this at all?

Looking back, I know how crazy this sounds, but that's what I did.

Ahhh—confession is so good for the soul!

But I don't regret it, not one single bite.

Earlier in the year, my brother, Jimmy, who was six years older than me, fell and was rushed to the hospital. The doctors discovered he had stage 4 lung cancer. It seemed to come out of nowhere. Looking back, I wonder, was it cancer or was it COVID? He had a lot of the same symptoms of COVID at the time, but the oncologist there diagnosed him with lung cancer. Jimmy's wife had passed a few years before his diagnosis, and his daughter, Monica, my niece, whom I love very much and am very close with, spent her winters with her daughter, competing in equestrian events in Wellington, Florida. As a result, she wasn't able to care for her father in person all the time. Neither she nor Helmut and I wanted Jimmy to be alone, as we both understood the importance of being there for him. Monica and I decided that when she couldn't be there, Helmut and I would be with Jimmy. Sadly, Jimmy lost his battle with cancer and passed in January 2020. It was a loss I didn't see coming and one I wasn't prepared for.

Monica was so good to her dad—and she, Helmut, and I were so glad we were there with Jimmy. My brother had many friends, and they surrounded him with love too. Jimmy had such a great sense of humor and always knew how to make me laugh. When I was a little girl, Jimmy let me read his comic books over his shoulder, leaning on him, without ever giving me a hard time. It was one of the ways I learned to read at such an early age. Jimmy was a wonderful big brother, who kept his infectious smile until the end.

Maybe it was losing Jimmy so quickly, or perhaps it was the uncertain state of the world during COVID, but I found myself being irrational about my symptoms, denying what was happening the way I had done the first time this happened. I can't even say it was denial. In that moment, it was my actual assessment of the situation.

It will go away.

It's nothing.

Wait and see.

Don't bother the good doctor.

I'm too busy.

It's too late at night.

I can't do this.

These are *all* sentences that could have a dire outcome.

The more I thought about it, the more ashamed I was.

Even so, I needed to get a third stent that night, and once again, Dr. Shlofmitz saved my life. Before leaving the hospital, I asked the doctor what I could do differently to ensure that we wouldn't be doing a fourth stent, especially because this time there was cholesterol.

Dr. Shlofmitz repeated what he had told me a few years earlier, assuring me that this was in my DNA. I wasn't sure if that made me feel better, but I decided to be more vigilant about my heart health in every way.

I spent the next few days convincing myself that I wouldn't say a word to anyone about this. But then, it occurred to me that there was great value in sharing what happened. If people understood that I knew better—that I even shared what I had learned along the way—they would also see the value in my telling them that even well-informed people on the subject can slip backward. In so many ways, I think I was ignoring the obvious out of habit. Like so many women, I believed every word I spoke that night. What I couldn't believe was that I had spent the prior three years being a heart health advocate and still fell into that trap. It was unintentional. It was automatic. This was a habit I needed to break before it broke me. Since this last scare, I am going to the cardiologist every six months as a precautionary measure. I have also requested a cardio CT to keep an eye on things. Depending on your risk factors, symptoms, and overall health, there are a number of tests to learn more about your heart health. Consult your physician and discuss your concerns. Becoming more proactive and aware of my heart health is extremely reassuring to me.

While I never expected to become a heart health advocate, I am grateful that I can use my platform to inform people about heart disease and treatment. What good is having the kind of reach I've been so blessed with if you can't use it to do some good in the world? I didn't put this all together when I first went to the hospital in 2018. And it wasn't the reason I called Jessica to see what she could do. I felt like a magnet was pulling me, compelling me to talk about it. Sometimes we get a calling in life. Perhaps it's not the one we were expecting, but it is hard to ignore. God always has a plan for us—it's up to us to act on it.

One final thought on health that I'd like to share is that many people don't know their complete family health history, and usually they don't think about it until they're in crisis, which is a very challenging time to start gathering that information. According to the American Heart Association (AHA), "Heart disease and stroke can affect a woman at any age, making it vital for all women to understand their personal risk factors and family history."[3] My father and grandmother both had heart attacks, but I never thought their conditions would impact me. Therefore, I never discussed that with Dr. Holly Andersen, my primary care physician and cardiologist. During my annual exam, she would listen to my heart and do routine blood work and an EKG, which always appeared normal and came back within the recommended margins. Dr. Andersen would assure me I was in excellent health because she had no reason to think otherwise or recommend heart imaging of any kind. If you're a person who knows your family history, make it a point to share that information with all your doctors. If I had done that with Dr. Andersen, I have no doubt she would have taken some precautions. So, when I found myself in the emergency room, Dr. Shlofmitz was in contact with Dr. Andersen to gather more information. Needless to say, she was as surprised as we all were. If you hear just one thing from this story, let it be this: *It can happen to anyone.*

I've talked a little bit about gratitude and joy, and the role each has played for me. I can think of no greater example of that in my life than the gratitude and joy I have for the opportunity to share my heart experience and pass it forward so that somebody—even if it is just one person—might hear it, triggering a light to go off in them and potentially saving their life. Knowing I can have this positive, potentially lifesaving impact on others, well, *that* is great joy.

When I went public with my heart condition, I did it for this very reason—to spread awareness and make an impact. What I never expected was the onslaught of people who came up to me afterward, and even to this day, saying that my story propelled them to go to the doctor and get a checkup.

Not long ago, I was in Bergdorf Goodman, my favorite department store in New York, contemplating buying a beautiful designer jacket. I didn't go into the store with the intention of spending so much money, but the jacket was just gorgeous. Like most of us, I began justifying the purchase, saying things like, "Colder weather is coming" and "This would be so nice to wear to lunch or dinner." I didn't mean to splurge like that (at least that's what I always told my husband). To be candid, I am no stranger to buying beautiful things. I believe in timeless pieces that I can keep for years. (I may have learned this from my mother, who also taught me to keep the shopping bags in the trunk of the car until Daddy went to work!)

Anyway, as I was thinking about buying this jacket, I noticed a very petite, attractive, blonde woman who was trying on the same jacket. She looked great in it. Well, that was all the confirmation I needed. I bought the jacket on the spot.

I took the piece home, hung it in my closet, and never wore it. Not once. That winter never got cold in New York, and when I tried the jacket on again at home, it didn't look nearly as good on me as it had on the other woman, even though we were built the same. It wasn't something that could be altered, and I knew I'd never wear it, so a few months later, I thought, *Maybe I'll take it back and exchange it for something I will wear.* I wasn't looking for a refund, but the jacket still had the tags on it, and I hoped the store would honor an exchange. I am embarrassed to admit this, but that was the first time in my life I had been to the service department at the fabulous Bergdorf's. That's code for "I never return anything there!"

When I got to the service department on the lower floor of the store, there was a woman ahead of me. While she was waiting, she turned to me and said, "This is the first time I've ever returned anything to Bergdorf Goodman."

"Me too!" I said with a laugh.

We couldn't believe it. It was such a funny thing to connect over. But then, she started to tell me about how she had seen me tell my heart story and that it had helped her so much because her husband was having some concerns.

"He's right over there," she said, pointing to him sitting off to the side with the other husbands. "He doesn't look like a heart patient. He's fit and appears to be the picture of health. But he hasn't been quite right lately. Because of you, I knew I needed to take him to see a doctor. He didn't want to go, but I insisted. In fact, we just came from there, and now here I am, standing in line at Bergdorf's with you!" she said with a smile.

She was so happy that he had gone for a checkup. They were waiting for the results, but she felt so good being proactive.

When she finished her return, we said our goodbyes. I wished her well and prayed everything would be fine.

I made my exchange (they honored it!), although it took a little while to happen. While I was waiting, the woman came back, only this time, with her husband. She was right. He was tall, slim, and looked like a healthy man. She wanted me to see him and see that he was taking the advice I shared about getting checked when something doesn't feel right. They were doing this together, which I loved. As it turns out, he was also a fan of *All My Children*. People are often surprised to learn that the show had a large male following—from boys in college to professional athletes, a lot of men watched and loved the show.

I was so touched by their gratitude, and it felt good knowing I had helped them in some small way.

According to the AHA, these ten essential facts are essential to know about women and cardiovascular disease:

1. Cardiovascular disease kills more women than all forms of cancer combined and yet only 44% of women recognize that cardiovascular disease is their greatest health threat.
2. Among females 20 years and older, nearly 45% are living with some form of cardiovascular disease and less than 50% of women entering pregnancy in the United States have good heart health.
3. Cardiovascular disease is the No. 1 killer of new moms and accounts for over one-third of maternal deaths. Black women have some of the highest maternal mortality rates.
4. Overall, 10% to 20% of women will have a health issue during pregnancy, and high blood pressure, preeclampsia, and gestational diabetes during pregnancy greatly increase a woman's risk for developing cardiovascular disease later in life.
5. Going through menopause does not cause cardiovascular disease, but the approach of menopause marks a point in midlife when women's cardiovascular risk factors can accelerate, making increased focus on health during this pivotal life stage crucial.
6. Most cardiac and stroke events can be prevented through education and lifestyle changes, such as moving more, eating smart and managing blood pressure.
7. 51.9% of high blood pressure deaths, otherwise known as hypertension or the "silent killer," are in women, and out of all women, 57.6% of Black females have hypertension—more than any other race or ethnicity.

8. While there are an estimated 4.1 million female stroke survivors living today, approximately 57.5% of total stroke deaths are in women.
9. Women are often less likely to receive bystander CPR because rescuers often fear accusations of inappropriate touching, sexual assault or injuring the victim.
10. Women continue to be underrepresented in Science, Technology, Engineering and Math (STEM) fields, as well as in research. In fact, women occupy nearly half of all U.S. jobs (48%), but only 27% of jobs in STEM fields. Furthermore, only 38% of participants in clinical cardiovascular trials are women.

*Accredited to American Heart Association and GoRedforWomen.org[4]

One last thought: Something I would like to accomplish in my work with the American Heart Association is to have the funding for research into women's heart health reach the same amount being spent on men's heart health. A study analyzing National Institutes of Health (NIH) funding from 2008 to 2019 identified 10,685 coronary artery disease projects, with only 4.5 percent (approximately $20.1 million) focused on women's heart health.[5] This equates to spending four dollars per man compared to just *seventeen cents* per woman! This feels so wrong. It *is* wrong. I certainly want men's heart health research to be funded, but I want women's heart health research to be equally funded. This just doesn't make any sense to me. As a result, I will commit to using my voice and my platform to help advocate for this change.

Chapter Eleven:

HOW AM I SUPPOSED TO LIVE WITHOUT YOU?

They say that pain is the price we pay for love. Well, the pain is excruciating, but I wouldn't give up even one second of the love.

—SUSAN LUCCI

Helmut was a passionate skier and golfer for many years. About a year and a half before his stroke, he was having some issues with his IT band. The IT (iliotibial) band is a thick, fibrous swathe of connective tissue that runs along the outside of the thigh, from the hip (ilium) to the bone just below the knee (tibia). It plays a crucial role in stabilizing the knee and supporting hip movement during activities like walking, running, skiing, and golfing. Tall men, especially golfers, also tend to have trouble with the L4 and L5 discs in their spine. I suppose it's all of that twisting that eventually takes a toll on the body, and the pain had become a nuisance to him. He wasn't able to play as much golf as he once did. It just wasn't as pleasurable for him anymore because of the chronic pain he was in—although Helmut never complained. He would always say, "It's like a car. Sometimes the parts need repair. The muffler breaks, you get it fixed. The brakes go, you take it into the shop."

Helmut sought medical advice and did everything he could to get back on the golf course. In fact, his conditions were treated so well, he had been given the okay by several of his doctors to go skiing in Austria with the family for Christmas in 2021. We always looked forward to our time together, and our times in Austria were particularly special. We loved to stay at the Hotel Post in Lech, a magical winter wonderland. I was thrilled to think this would be okay for him, as Helmut skied like the wind and was as graceful as a dancer—always so smooth and fast and gorgeous to watch. I was so happy, too, that his children—and little grandchildren—would see him and have fun with him in his "natural habitat."

"I am so happy the doctors have given you the okay. I know we will have a great time, but please promise me you won't go right to the double black diamond runs. At least do a couple of warm-up runs before you do," I said with a tone of seriousness wrapped in a great big smile.

A few years before this planned trip, Helmut had a fall during another ski trip. That time, we were in Utah, staying at the Stein Eriksen Lodge. Usually, Helmut and Andreas would ski together because they were both spectacular skiers. I was never a skier in the same breadth or category as they were. But I did want to ski, and whenever Helmut and I skied together, I would follow him down the mountain. Doing this removed a lot of my fear because he knew where we were going. I could just follow him, get into the swing of it, relax, and have fun.

We decided to get up early one morning, have breakfast, and go to the ski room. The Stein Eriksen Lodge is known for their lavish customer service. They store your skis and, in the morning, have all your gear ready, including your boots, which have been prewarmed. They practically brush your hair for you as you walk through the lobby! I'll admit, it's fabulous, and it sure does add to the experience of being on that mountain. Anyway, we figured we could get a few runs in, and then he could join Andreas and his friend in the afternoon. We had just finished breakfast and were making our way to the ski room. Helmut, who was walking in front of me, went out onto the wooden porch, which had two or three steps leading to the asphalt below.

Helmut kidded around a lot. He was always saying or doing

something to make people laugh. He was just a fun man to be around. He was walking in kind of a funny way, and I thought, *Oh, he skis like the wind and is now playfully walking. He's just fooling around.*

But he wasn't fooling around.

Helmut lost his balance and fell. I don't know if he slipped on something, but he went flying over the steps, never touching one of them, and landed on the concrete sidewalk. He was bleeding, and I thought he was unconscious. I started calling for help, but it was so early in the morning, nobody was around who could hear me, so I ran back into the lodge. Fortunately, the concierge desk happened to be right next to the door. I wanted to remain calm and didn't want to call too much attention to the scene, but the worst-case scenario was going through my mind. I wanted to scream, but somehow I held on to my composure.

"Help! Help! My husband just fell," I said.

The concierge couldn't have been more responsive. He told me he'd call an ambulance and get Helmut the help he needed.

When I knew I had gotten my message across and was confident they were getting help, I ran back outside. While I was inside, a bicyclist taking a morning ride in the mountains saw Helmut and stopped.

He looked up and said to me, "He's conscious. He's going to be okay."

By the time he uttered those words, the ambulance pulled up. It felt like nothing short of miraculous because I really thought he had seriously injured himself—or worse.

We went to the hospital, where they asked him several questions, wanting to know if he had blacked out. He didn't present as if he had. And it didn't appear as though he'd had any kind of ministroke. We didn't know what had happened.

The paramedics and doctors focused on Helmut's heart and the fact that he had A-fib because his blood pressure was very high after the fall and from the altitude. Although Helmut hadn't hit his head that morning, he had hit his face on the concrete. He looked like he had been in a fight with a pack of wild dogs—and lost. Thank goodness he'd tried to break his fall by putting his hand down quickly to protect his head.

We learned that when he landed, he tore his rotator cuff in five places and sprained his wrist. He had two slings, one from his shoulder and the other from the hand that went down to protect his wrist. Once he was bandaged up and they were able to get his blood pressure under control, they released him.

The next night, his heart began pounding a mile a minute as his blood pressure went up to alarming levels once again. Concerned, to say the least, we went back to the hospital, where they asked if there had been any recent falls aside from the one he'd taken the day before. Sure enough, as we were getting ready to go on this trip, Helmut had gone up to the attic, where we stored our suitcases. When he was coming down, he missed the last step, which was the same color as the wood floor beneath it. (I had always meant to put something on that step, like red nail polish, to make it stand out more, but I never did.) And, of course, Helmut fell. He was a big man, standing six feet two. Luckily, he did not hit his head or sustain a head injury, so we didn't really think about it when he fell at the lodge. Nobody seemed alarmed when we told them about this fall. Needless to say, his accident cut our trip short. I was completely fine with that. I just wanted to go home and make sure Helmut was okay.

We were living in Los Angeles at the time as *All My Children* had been moved to the West Coast. We hadn't been there long and had no relationship with any local doctors. The husband of one of the directors I worked with practiced at Cedars-Sinai. I loved this director. She was so talented and very kind. And I trusted her. So, I asked if her husband might have a referral for someone to treat Helmut's rotator cuff. Thankfully, he did. She sent us to Dr. Neal ElAttrache, an orthopedic surgeon whom she described as the very best doctor and movie-star handsome. As always, I wanted to do my own due diligence, so I called our good friend, Dr. Steve O'Brien, an accomplished orthopedic surgeon at the Hospital for Special Surgery (HSS) in New York, to get his opinion. He picked up the phone right away and wholeheartedly agreed that Dr. ElAttrache would be his first choice in Los Angeles.

Dr. ElAttrache did the surgery, which was followed by a long recuperation, and I learned a lot. Helmut eventually regained his range of motion, which took several months and a lot of physical therapy. He was a trooper every step of the way.

For many years after this, our lives continued as normal. But Helmut had A-fib and decided to have an ablation, a minimally invasive procedure used to treat abnormal electrical short circuits in the heart. He continued to have A-fib. The ablation never took effect, so his heart irregularity persisted. But Helmut never had any symptoms or limitations from his A-fib, so I must say that we were incredibly lucky to travel and ski and do whatever we wanted to—until we couldn't.

Three months before Helmut passed, I came home to find him already back from the office for the evening. It was an especially cold January night, and he was standing in front of the fireplace in our kitchen trying to get warm.

"I feel a little funny in my arms. They've felt weak all day," he said.

Again, this was a man who never—and I mean *never*—complained about anything. He was just telling me how strange it felt. Neither one of us thought much about it. Then he said, "Sometimes, I was feeling that a little bit in my legs today too. It's very strange."

Even so, Helmut went out to pick up dinner from one of our favorite Italian restaurants. While he was out, I set the table. We both sat down and ate dinner like any other evening at home. I got up to clear the dishes. I was standing over the sink when I noticed Helmut get up, then go down like a house of cards. Again, he didn't hit his head. He didn't appear to lose consciousness. Concerned but not panicked, we called his cardiologist, Dr. Richard Shlofmitz, the same doctor who saved my life and put the stents in. He said to call an ambulance, and he'd meet us at the hospital.

The ambulance arrived, although I wish it hadn't taken so long. We went to the hospital, and they were certain he hadn't had a stroke. He didn't present as a stroke victim. There was no slurring of speech. He was lucid. There was no drooping on one side of his face. Dr. Shlofmitz ordered an MRI and a brain scan to be certain.

After that, Helmut started walking with a cane because he didn't feel like his balance was steady anymore. He had been going to physical therapy, and they kept reassuring him that his balance was getting better. And I could see the improvement myself. I had gone to all his sessions with him, and I thought he was getting stronger and steadier. But he didn't agree. He knew he wasn't walking as solidly as he had been a few months earlier.

Helmut was always managing projects around our home. He wanted a certain planting of trees removed from our property. He walked down the lawn with his cane to talk with the men who were doing the work. A week later, on February 27, he walked down again to check the progress. I wasn't home; I was so convinced that Helmut was doing great, I had made plans to go to New York City. It was the first time I had been in the city for months. When I arrived at my meeting, my phone rang, and it was Helmut. I was so surprised to hear the way he was speaking. He was slurring his words, mumbling, "I think I had a stroke."

"I'll be right there," I said.

Thank God, I made it from Sixty-First and Fifth in Manhattan to NYU Langone Hospital in Long Island in thirty-one minutes. That had to be some kind of speed record.

I got there in time to follow the ambulance to the emergency room. Andreas was walking in with Helmut. In the meantime, I had spoken to one of the men who was with Helmut when he had the stroke. He said that Helmut had walked down to see the progress they were making just as he had done the week before, but when he turned around to walk back to the house, Helmut appeared to lose his balance. Thank goodness, those two men were there because they were able to catch him and walk him back to the house. Of course, Helmut protested. He said he didn't need help, even though he did. When they got to the house, Helmut was saying he wanted to go to St. Francis Hospital, the world-renowned heart hospital where I had also been treated.

"Mrs. Huber. He needs to go to the nearest hospital," one of the men said.

I could hear the man's voice trembling.

When it comes to a stroke, time is of the essence. And while the ambulance took nearly a half hour to arrive, we were losing precious time.

Once we arrived at the hospital, they immediately took him to the emergency room. He was sitting up while they asked him *those* questions.

"Do you know where you are?"

"Do you know what day it is?"

"Do you know who this is?" as they pointed to Andreas.

"My son," Helmut said.

"And do you know who this is?" pointing to me.

"My wife."

He was lucid, which I thought was a good sign.

In the meantime, Andreas and I were called into another room, where we met two surgeons, who gave us their opinion on the situation.

"I'm sorry, I don't know your credentials. Are you really good at this?" I asked.

I wasn't trying to be rude or insulting, and thankfully, the head surgeon, who was the chief operating surgeon, wasn't offended by my question. He didn't start bragging or selling me on his capabilities. He calmly and empathetically reassured me that he does this type of surgery every day. He was kindhearted and exceptionally gentle with his words.

The other surgeon was a big burly man who spoke with a slight Irish accent. His bedside manner was gruffer than his colleague's.

"It would be foolish to expect a full recovery because he is eighty-four years old," he said in a no-nonsense, straight-talking way.

"That number does not define him," I said.

"Don't think about that. My father is strong and incredibly resilient," Andreas said.

All I could think of in that moment was being strong for Helmut . . . and what a great son we shared. Andreas and I did our best to explain that Helmut was a dynamic man who had just been given the okay to ski in the Alps of Austria.

"This is a strong man. Please, please help save him," I said in a tone just slightly over a whisper.

Finally, Andreas and I were both thinking, *Let's just stop talking and go do the surgery! Let's go!*

After the surgery, both doctors came out to tell Andreas and me that it had gone extremely well. Helmut was able to respond to the clinical tests they were doing, which was promising. Helmut could follow the doctor's finger with his eyes. He followed my voice. He knew me. He could do all the things with his hands and feet that they were asking him to do.

The first day, we had every hope.

By the second day, however, he wasn't responding quite as much.

On the third day, even less.

It was around day three that the doctors induced a coma to help resolve the bleeding that was happening in his brain. Unfortunately, he never came out of it.

I can't say enough about these incredible doctors. The team of professionals treating Helmut was terrific with us. We met with them every morning. The physician's assistants were so informative and smart. Every nurse on every shift was wonderful, caring, and nurturing. No one rushed me to make any decisions. In so many ways, I was fortunate because Helmut was in such good hands.

I reached out to our friend, Dr. Dan Barrow, a renowned neurosurgeon and head of neurology at Emory in Atlanta. So much was coming at me from everyone and from every direction, I felt as though I needed a logical voice of reason I could talk to, trust, and ask questions of. The doctors at NYU Langone–Long Island were wonderful, but I just didn't know them, and they didn't know Helmut. I can never thank Dan Barrow enough. Dan made himself available whenever I needed him. He would talk to me late at night, early in the morning—it didn't matter. He spoke with the doctors at the hospital, who all knew his name and reputation, and they conferred on Helmut's MRI results and other tests, working beautifully together as a team. Everyone was so good at what they did, and they were so patient and kind in answering all of my and Andreas's many questions.

I spent the whole month of March with Helmut, and I am forever grateful for the time I had with him every day. I felt lucky to share that time together. One of the nurses told me about a television channel I could put on in his room that played beautiful, peaceful music along with images of exquisite landscapes from all around the world. Often, they were in the mountains, whether it was winter, spring, summer, or fall. They showed the snow caps in the Alps and the meadows with the mountain flowers blooming. Helmut always loved that. I held his hand and talked to him, telling him about what I was seeing. And I knew he could hear me.

I think . . . I hope . . . he could envision what I was describing.

These were places we had been, skied, and vacationed at as a family—places he loved. As I've said before, there are no coincidences. Why would these beautiful mountains in his home country, where he grew up, be flashing on the screen? He was being called home, and I never wanted to let go of his hand.

I read the sports pages to him every morning. On the weekends I put the golf tournaments on and told him who was on the leaderboard. I played the beautiful, incredible music of Andrea Bocelli and the wonderful Charles Aznavour, a French singer Helmut had introduced me to and taken me to see. When I heard him singing one of his beautiful love songs, I was overwhelmed with the desire to put my arms around Helmut—and I did. And then I walked around to the other side of his bed, put my arms around him, laid my head on his chest, and danced with him. And I am so profoundly grateful I did . . . I'm so thankful that I followed my instincts.

The hospital was gracious to allow me to sleep in the Barcalounger in his room, so he was never alone. Every once in a while, they'd convince me to go home, but it was rare and for a very short time because I was so afraid he was going to die, and I didn't want him to die alone. I wanted to be with him. I didn't want to leave him. And I didn't want him to leave.

As the weeks went on, it had become apparent that there was absolutely no hope that Helmut would recover. Again, nobody rushed us to make any decisions, and no one ever stopped talking to me, answering the questions Andreas and I continuously asked. I felt so incredibly supported.

Early one morning, it was still dark outside, I was sitting with Helmut in the ICU, when one of the surgeons who had treated Helmut—the big burly one with the straight-talking bedside manner—walked into the room. Without saying a word, he took my hand and placed a rosary in it. I was so touched by this gesture. It made me feel as though there was an extra blessing on Helmut—and our family.

One of the doctors told me there was hospice care within the hospital, which is what I chose to have. I struggled with that decision—about a week before, Andreas and I thought we saw Helmut's eyelids flutter when he heard Andreas's voice. Andreas and I asked the doctors if they could do just one more exam, including an MRI to confirm that hospice was the right decision. And indeed, it was. I knew how excellent the quality of care would be from the hospice nurses right there at the hospital. I didn't want to move him. I also felt it would be less wear and tear on Helmut. I knew he would have the same spectacular care in hospice as he did in the ICU. And indeed, he did.

He fought so hard. I know he tried to live. I could see it.

But he didn't make it.

Helmut passed away around two a.m. on March 28.

Andreas and I were by his side.

I was lying next to him.

After losing Helmut, I would see other couples walking together holding hands everywhere I went—and I ached to have Helmut walking with me, holding hands. I was so genuinely happy that these couples still had each other—but after Helmut passed, it felt as though I were in a dream state. I looked at everyone around me and thought how vulnerable we all are. I wondered, *Is this life even real? What is it all about?*

Every question slowly chipped away at my sense of being whole. I never imagined that I'd someday find myself making arrangements for my husband's funeral. I had been to the Fairchild Funeral Home many, many (too many) times for visitations, but I never once thought the day would come when I would be the person having visitation services. I couldn't say the word *wake.*

And then I realized that grief is not something you can really understand until you go through it—until you experience it. Until it's *your* grief and *you're* sitting in the front row at the funeral. That's when you understand that what you're experiencing is not *a* moment in time. It's not a broken bone that will heal. It is something that is permanent. That's the moment you come to understand that some things can't be fixed. They just can't. And I guess there is a sense of peace knowing that, and of course, there is also pain. Everyone is different, but it's a horrendous process.

There was so much to coordinate, as anybody who has been through this knows. We wanted to have the funeral and the celebration of life on the same day. I wasn't ready to say these unimaginable words out loud: *casket* and *funeral.* As hard as it was, the funeral director and staff somehow made it bearable for me with their kindness and sensitivity. Andreas was with me, and they could not have been kinder to us.

Helmut's son from his first marriage, Dany, and Andreas were pallbearers, along with two of Helmut's grown grandsons, Christian and Simon. To see these strapping, handsome young men, who each adored Helmut, together was lovely. When I closed my eyes, I could see Dany, who was nineteen when Andreas was two, running around our yard playing soccer. Dany played soccer for a semipro team in Zürich. He could do so many tricks with the soccer ball. As a young boy, Andreas idolized him. They have remained friends all this time, which I know made Helmut very happy. Dany's wife, Mirella, whom I have always loved, called me almost every day during the month of March while Helmut was in the hospital, and she and I walked down the aisle behind Helmut's casket, holding on to each other. I was also so grateful that my daughter-in-law, Courtney, stayed by my side during the entire time of Helmut's wake.

You're not allowed to give a eulogy in our Catholic church, but immediately following the services, we went to the Garden City Hotel, where we had celebrated so many of our happy life events, including first communions and confirmations and our daughter Liza's wedding reception. And now, I was listening to our son give the most gorgeous, heartfelt, and beautifully constructed eulogy for his dad. So many of our friends and Andreas's friends spoke so lovingly about Helmut too. Many of them did a very good imitation of Helmut, with his adorable Austrian accent, recounting so many wonderful stories filled with love and humor, which I loved hearing. I knew Helmut would be proud—and proud of the food we served too. We chose all his favorites—foods Helmut would have wanted and chosen for himself.

When the funeral was over and the celebration of life was behind me, I was left with nothing but my thoughts, my sadness, and my grief.

I couldn't imagine living without Helmut.

I . . . could . . . not . . . imagine . . . it.

I sometimes still wonder, *How is it that I am living and he is gone?*

I was aware that the process of reconciling the tsunami of emotions I was carrying would be long. And I also came to the conclusion that I didn't want to thumb my nose at or not be grateful for this gift of life that God has given me. It's meant to be a gift, not to be taken for granted. As I contemplated what would come next, I remembered something my mother used to say: "God wants us to be happy."

This would take time; of that I was certain.

And it would require a level of resilience, something I wasn't sure would ever be a part of my life again.

Helmut was incredibly resilient. Growing up during World War II, he ran to bomb shelters with his mother when he was just two years old. I think when you've seen the worst of humanity and have grown up around that, you've also witnessed the best of humanity, as people with resilience rebuild and move forward with their lives.

Maybe when you've experienced horrible things, you find the strength and courage to live to see another day. Maybe that's what makes you roll with things. I don't know the answer. Not now, and certainly not then. I would sometimes say to Helmut, "You're so much more evolved than I am." He just always seemed to have it together. Without his light, his guidance, how would I go on?

What I did know was that I was going to have to dig incredibly deep to be able to move forward—to be able to stay standing. I would just take things one day at a time.

Chapter Twelve:

THERE MUST BE A CRACK IN THE UNIVERSE

It's only when you get beyond the emotion of fear and move into the unknown—despite the fear—that you turn your fear into passion and courage.

—DR. JOE DISPENZA

I am a romantic. My husband, Helmut, was a realist. He was confident and full of ease in navigating the world. I adored him. I also admired him. And I learned so much from him. As they say on the golf course, we ham-and-egged it. We each brought something to the table. We came from different parts of the world, different generations, different cultures, different backgrounds. And yet we had so much in common. We couldn't stop talking to each other. He was never timid, but I know he was afraid at the end, and that kills me down to my soul.

When Helmut died, a big piece of me died too. We had been married since I was twenty-two years old. He was the great love of my life. I fell more and more in love with him the longer we were together. I wasn't sure how to be on my own in the world or whether I would ever step foot on a stage or in front of a camera again.

For me, part of healing was deciding to make a choice to put one foot in front of the other. It didn't happen right away, but it does get a little easier with time. And the thing is—I did that, and I'm still doing it!

I am keenly aware that I have been given the gift of life, that God gives this, and I don't ever want to thumb my nose at that tremendous gift. I want to do the best I can with the gift of life I have been given. Choosing not to be sad all the time, to the extent I can, is a better choice than lying in a puddle on the floor. I have had my share of those days and nights when grief washed over me like a tidal wave. But some days became gentler than others. It hasn't been a straight line to healing. One moment I was fine, and the next I was breaking down. There are still days when I am not sure which it will be. And that's okay. But I am learning to recognize it, acknowledge it, and feel it. I'm learning to cope, one day at a time.

I started reading—a lot. Friends suggested or sent books that had helped them, and I found them to be helpful too. There were many books from people with various backgrounds that talked a lot about grief, healing, and gratitude.

What I've come to understand about grief is that it's deeply personal—no two journeys are the same. There's no rulebook, no timeline, no "right" way to feel. It arrives on its own terms, often unannounced. You can't plan for it, push it aside, outsleep it, or outrun it. No amount of distraction or exhaustion will make it disappear. Grief lingers in the quiet moments, weaves itself into the everyday, and when it washes over you, it doesn't ask permission—it simply is.

Learning how to be in my grief but not be permanently paralyzed by it has been a piece of the healing process. It's not easy, but that is how it has been for me.

A few months before Helmut died, I had committed to perform in *Celebrity Autobiography*, the hilarious play created by the ingenious Eugene Pack and Dayle Reyfel, in which celebrities read passages from other celebrities' autobiographies. While I had canceled every other obligation I had, for whatever reason, I didn't cancel this appearance. I'd done the show numerous times and had always enjoyed being part of the revolving ensemble cast. As the date drew closer, I knew I had to try to put one foot in front of the other. I was in search of myself, and finally I realized how lucky I am to have my work to go to.

I've always loved performing; it's who I am to my core. I wanted to feel this again.

I'm going to do this, I thought to myself.

I knew the material, and it's a funny show. A little laughter couldn't hurt, right? No doubt, the other cast members would make me laugh, and that would be very good for my heart and soul. That night, I would be performing with the hilariously talented Mario Cantone. I just look at Mario and I'm in stitches. Richard Kind, Brooke Shields, Alan Zweibel, and Eugene Pack were also there. All of these people are amazing to work with and can make me laugh at the drop of a hat. Hopefully, I'd muster up the ability to make them and the audience laugh too.

The show was at Adelphi University, which is very close to where I live, making it a lot easier for me to do it. Even so, I remember thinking, *How will I ever step on that stage, especially in my hometown, where all of my friends will no doubt be there to support me?* I knew I would feel the audience's love and care. I didn't want to lose it or break down on stage. This thought ran on a constant loop in my mind until the night of the show. But then I reminded myself that the people in the audience were there to have a good time. They were not there to see me cry—they were there for us to make them laugh. If I ever compartmentalized in my life, it was surely that night. It was the only way I'd get through it. Although I was very nervous, as it turned out, doing this was really good for me. I had butterflies as I went over the material for the evening. I had to keep my focus on my work. Thankfully, none of the actors offered their condolences beforehand. We had a show to do, and I know they understood that, professionally, I needed to be in the right mindset to pull this off. I appreciated their thoughtfulness and understanding more than they knew. I am certain if just one person had said they were sorry for my loss, I would not have been able to go on. Helmut had always been with me when I went on stage. But he wasn't there.

He wasn't there.

I didn't know how I could do this.

I'll admit, there were many times as an actor I'd questioned whether I could play a part or do it well. I'd doubt myself, over and over, unsure if I was capable. It wasn't an act. In those moments, I genuinely felt that way. Helmut was always there to say, "You can do this with one hand tied behind your back. Of course you can. Go on, go out there. Go!" Hearing him say that would give me the courage to believe I could do anything. I never took that encouragement for granted. I was always so happy when Helmut cheered me on. I heard his words in my head and in my heart, and it gave me the strength to go out there and give it my all. I am 100 percent sure that was what he would have wanted me to do—and what I wanted to do, to accomplish.

And so, I did.

It took every fiber of my being to keep it together when I walked onto that stage because the audience was so incredibly warm and welcoming. I was so very grateful to feel their presence. But I didn't want to cry. Just six weeks earlier, I hadn't believed I'd ever be able to do this. I hadn't even thought it would matter as much as it did.

Helmut had always been there on nights like this. He was constantly by my side for these performances. He'd scan the house, sit through the sound check, and support me in every way. Afterward, we'd go out for a late dinner and a glass of champagne with friends and recap the show before going home. I missed him like crazy, but I also knew he'd be cheering for me.

"The show must go on."

After that performance, it became even clearer to me that I had so much opportunity ahead of me, and a place to go and do what I love to do—a place where I would enjoy some continuity in a good and creative way. I was lucky to have that because until that night—for a while anyway—I felt lost and scared that I wouldn't be able to do what I had done all my life. Realizing I'd be okay, that I *could* still perform, was a grace that has helped save me.

A few weeks later, Andreas, his wife, and their two little children were with me to celebrate Mother's Day.

I did my best to be in the moment that day, despite feeling the absence of my husband. Being with my family, especially my children and grandchildren, is a source of deep joy.

I was standing in line at the buffet when a friend of Helmut's came over to say hello. It was the first time I'd seen him since Helmut passed.

He stood there for a split second without saying a word. He looked at me directly in the eyes, and his words touched me so deeply. "There must be a crack in the universe with Helmut gone." His words said it all. I stood there in awe that he could put into words how I was feeling. This type of exchange was all so new to me. It was so wonderful to feel that kind of love for Helmut coming from outside of myself, from somebody else. I remember feeling numb at the time but not because of what he said or how he looked. I was deeply moved by that exchange. I thought it was such a beautiful way to express how he was feeling. Certainly, it expressed what I was feeling. How lovely that one of Helmut's colleagues and friends felt that way too. This man is not a poet, lyricist, or writer. He is someone who shared the same profession as my husband and who clearly had deep affection for him. The impact of his words was incredibly powerful. As I said earlier, words are so very powerful. They can build us up or tear us down. They can connect us or divide us. This man's words that day meant so much to me and my healing.

When Helmut passed, I felt like half a person. I struggled to get back to myself, wondering if I would ever feel like me again. Would I ever know myself again, the me I had always been? For a while there, it felt as though I were living in this awful space somewhere between the life I once had and the life I didn't ask for. It felt like a strange type of muscle memory, like I was still reaching for what was gone while the echoes of normalcy taunted me with what used to be. I knew my normal was no longer the same.

These feelings were foreign to me. I've always been a happy person. Joyful, strong, and resilient. I think I was born this way. Did my life experiences come to me because I was given the eyes and ears to see and hear things with a happy heart, strength, and resilience? Perhaps. And oh, yes, there was a lot of luck in there too. One thing is for sure, I always rolled with whatever life brought my way. I always considered myself to be a happy survivor and proud of how much I could withstand. How much I could tolerate.

Until now.

Until I lost Helmut.

Until my beautiful husband passed away.

I can hardly say the words *lost him*. It's just too painful. And to think I almost walked away from this love because once I fell for Helmut, I felt this despicable vulnerability. The thing I hated most about being in love was and is the vulnerability that came along with it. And yet, I loved Helmut. There was no denying that. And I didn't want to give him up. Helmut made no secret of how much he loved me. He made me laugh; he was so confident, so unafraid, so decisive. We were married within eight months of dating. But I made him promise that he would never come home to me just because he had a ring on his finger, so I learned to live with that overwhelming, despicable vulnerability. To love deeply means to be vulnerable to the sorrow of loss.

I thank God for creating Helmut Huber and for putting him on this earth—and in my life. My faith has been enormously important throughout my life, but especially during this time. I used to read stories about people who would say that if they didn't have their faith, they wouldn't have gotten through whatever hardship they were facing. Or that their faith saved them from despair. Before I went through any of this, I remember thinking, *How can anyone say that? God took that person away from them!* But how could I not be grateful for the love Helmut and I shared? For having him in my life? There's no doubt we had a wonderful relationship. We have two beautiful children and six wonderful grandchildren. We were healthy and happy, and we lived a very blessed and exciting life. I get it. I don't want you to feel sorry for me. In fact, I sometimes hear the song "Don't Cry for Me Argentina" in my inside voice when I write things like this. "And the truth is, I never . . ." once took any of this for granted.

Chapter Thirteen:

THE QUIET STRENGTH WITHIN

Your vision will become clear only when you can look into your heart. Who looks outside, dreams; who looks inside, awakens.

—CARL JUNG,

Memories, Dreams, Reflections

When I was a teenager, I remember reading an article about Rose Kennedy. In the piece, she talked about how her faith helped sustain her in the face of great tragedy and grief. She had so much tragedy in her life that, at the time, I remember thinking, *Really? With so much loss, wouldn't you lose your faith?* So many people she loved and cared about had been taken from her, and yet, there she was, talking about how her faith had helped her get through such unimaginable loss.

Mrs. Kennedy spoke about how she prayed to God, and when she did, he would come and sustain her, giving her peace and tranquility. I've never forgotten those powerful words or the strength in her beliefs. She went on to talk about how a mother shouldn't complain about her loss or be in tears all the time because she thought it was very bad for the family. As the mother of nine children, she understood the need to be pragmatic and to keep her family on that same path. She ended her interview by saying, "God intends us to be happy."[6] This amazed me because she said the same thing my mother had said to me!

Hearing this mother, this matriarch of the Kennedy family, speaking this way took my breath away. I didn't realize I had held on to those words for more than fifty years, but I had. It's quite remarkable to know that we can be so positively imprinted by something we read or hear without ever knowing it until we truly need that information.

I don't talk about my faith often. I personally feel that my relationship with God is a private and unshakable bond between him and me. And I am profoundly grateful for it. I have found throughout my life that my faith and the strength of that relationship has pulled me through to the other side of unimaginable darkness and has compelled me to share my thoughts on the subject with you now.

There were so many times I had to put my faith in God's hands, especially after Helmut had his stroke. When he was in the hospital, I was with him the whole time. Even though he was in a coma, the nurses let me sleep in his room, which I greatly appreciated. Even so, most nights, one of them would tell me to go home so I could get a good night's sleep—something that had eluded me since he went into the hospital. It was true that we only lived five minutes away, but I wanted to be right by his side, especially if anything were to happen.

"We'll call you. We promise," the nurses would say.

"I know you promise to call, and I believe you will, but it would take me five minutes to get here, and I don't want Helmut to die alone," I responded.

That's how I felt.

I sometimes flashed back to our son, Andreas, who had fought so hard to gain his strength from a terrible flu as a newborn baby. I think that was the first time I truly questioned my faith. I remember thinking if Andreas, as a baby, didn't live, I wasn't sure I could keep my faith. Why would a loving and caring God take a baby? It made no sense to me then, anymore than it does now. But my son lived, and I will never forget the words his doctor said to me back then. They were so powerful, they bear repeating—over and over, especially in times of being challenged:

"Don't ever underestimate the power of what you are doing. Your prayers and your presence are making a difference. The sensation of your touch and the soothing sound of your voice have tremendous healing power."

This is faith.

Of course, it was easy to keep my faith after Andreas survived in the NICU, though I know this is not always the outcome for people—and that's why I questioned it back then.

And why I questioned it again after losing Helmut.

In fact, I'd say that right after losing Helmut, I was momentarily angry with God for taking my husband away.

That anger didn't last, but it was how I felt at that time. And once my initial anger began to disappear, it quickly morphed into deep gratitude. I was and remain so grateful that I had this kind of love in my life. I know that doesn't come around every day of the week. How lucky I am to have known this love at all.

While I've heard many stories of people who felt as though they lost their faith when they suffered a great loss, that wasn't me. In fact, my faith was something I reached for and leaned on. If you lose a child, I understand that you could lose faith. Same with losing the love of your life; you could lose faith.

And for most of us, our first inclination is to ask why.

Why did this happen?

I came to believe that God has a divine plan.

I wish losing my husband wasn't part of that plan. But it was, and there was nothing I could do to change that truth or dull the pain I felt. Nothing except turn to and embrace my faith. Instead of questioning why, I chose to focus on my immense gratitude for the love of having Helmut in my life.

Helmut had a cornucopia of wonderful sayings. He'd drop them into a conversation when you least expected it. And the way he expressed himself was charming beyond belief. On our first date, he shared a few memorable quips with me, including this Austrian proverb: "As you call into the forest, so the echo comes back to you."

After Helmut died, I had not really dreamed about him. But then,

I did. I had a dream about him that woke me from my sleep. I sat up in the middle of the night and thought, *Was it* just *a dream?*

It rattled me to my core. I had to write about it right then and there. I turned on the light, and the words just poured out of me at two a.m.

It has been one year and four months since he died. I can hardly write the word. I have to pause to take a breath and force my hand to write the word "died." In my dream, Helmut and I were walking along together. Happy. Happy. The next thing I knew, he was way on top of a mountain, an enormous hill hundreds of feet above me on my left. I wanted to climb up to him. I didn't know how we got separated.

Had I taken a wrong turn?

Taken the wrong road?

As I kept walking, I hoped he would come down to me. And then I realized that the mountain was soft—it was sand. It would collapse. It would swallow him up if he tried to walk down or slide down to me. I realized that I couldn't climb up to him. The sand would not give me my footing. It would not let me climb up to him. So I kept on walking, keeping my eyes on him, hoping I would find a path up to him.

I had our toddler with us, and suddenly we were walking in the woods. It was dark and green, like a deep forest or jungle. And our toddler fell into a pond, or a lake. It was a dark pool of water. I was horrified. I was terrified. I immediately reached in, grabbed him, and miraculously pulled him out. He was wet and shivering, but alive. I tried to dry him off to keep him warm . . . to get him warm. I took him by the hand and turned around to go back to where we got separated from Helmut. I would look for the road. I would try to find our way up to Helmut on top of that sand mountain, hundreds of feet above us, where I had seen him walking easily on top. But I woke up. I didn't get to him.

When I first had this dream, I didn't know how to interpret it. I thought maybe it was just a dream. And then, while writing this book, it occurred to me that there was no way to get him back. It was a means of dealing with the finality of his passing and making sure our children were going to be okay.

I think that dreams have a mysterious way of delivering important messages just when we need them most, somehow acting as a bridge between our conscious and subconscious minds. In the quiet stillness of sleep, when the noise of daily life fades away, our minds can tap into deeper insights and emotions that we might overlook while awake. These messages often come in symbolic or unexpected forms—a vivid image, a recurring theme, or even a seemingly random scenario—that resonate with our inner struggles, hopes, or unanswered questions. It's as if our subconscious knows exactly what we need to process or understand, offering clarity, guidance, or even comfort in moments of uncertainty. I think dreams are maybe one of the wonderful mysteries of life.

Whether dreams come from God, faith, or the subconscious mind is a deeply personal question that depends on our own beliefs and perspectives. Many people of faith view dreams as a form of divine communication, a way for God to offer guidance, warnings, or encouragement. Ultimately, I think they can offer profound insights and serve as a source of inspiration, healing, and clarity when we choose to pay attention to them.

I start my mornings and end my evenings by praying in gratitude. This helps keep me spiritually connected and reminds me I am not alone. It also helps me set my day with intentionality. To start and end each day with a full heart and the notion of doing good—of being the best human I can possibly be—in gratitude for this gift of life God has given me.

During my grief, I have found my faith to be a source of strength and guidance, a quiet reminder that there is still love, resilience, hope, and a role to fulfill.

There is no doubt that if it weren't for my faith, I would not be here sharing my innermost thoughts with you. Why do I say that? With so much gratitude and love in my heart, I feel a pull, a draw, to want to give back. I am so lucky to have this platform, to share my life and experiences with you, and to have faith—yes, deep faith—that by doing so, I am serving a higher purpose. Look, I didn't plan to have a near-fatal heart condition in 2018 either, but from that experience, it became very clear to me that I needed to pass my good fortune on. I could not keep it to myself. I was given the opportunity to share critical information and resources to help others.

The Christmas before Helmut passed, he gave me a necklace with three charms that read, "Hope," "Love," and "Joy."

After his passing, I couldn't wear it because there was no hope or joy. Only love.

I couldn't even say the word *hope.* After Helmut died, the only thing I hoped for was that Helmut would come walking through the door again, but of course, that was not possible.

At that point, I felt all hope was gone.

How do I go forward without hope?

How do I regain faith and hope?

While I eventually learned that *all* hope is not taken away, nothing else really mattered to me. Helmut's passing was all I thought about. But somehow, even when I was having moments of hopelessness and devastation, I still clung to my faith.

Right before Helmut passed away, it became clear that I had to arrange for him to be given last rites. I remembered Monsignor James Vlaun, whom Helmut and I had met many times over the years while doing his telethons. He was always jolly, and I said to Andreas, "Monsignor Vlaun is just who we need. We need his jolly presence."

Monsignor Vlaun came and gave Helmut last rites and prayed with Andreas and me. And he ended up presiding over the services we had for Helmut.

About a month after Helmut passed away, I had lunch with Monsignor Vlaun. I shared that I had done a lot of reading about life after death and asked him if he believed in such a thing.

"Of course," he answered sincerely and quite convincingly.

I knew I was speaking with a man of religion. This is his life. He's chosen to do what he does, so even before asking him, I knew what he would say.

"Do you believe that I am going to be reunited with Helmut, that I am going to see him again?"

Without batting an eyelash, he said, "Yes, of course. That's the promise. You will know them, and they shall know you."

"I know you are a man of great faith and a man of religion, and of course that's what you're going to say to me, but I need to know this. Is Helmut going to be like this ether? Because I just want to put my arms around him." I felt so raw sharing this with the monsignor.

"You will be able to," he gently responded.

I just needed to keep my faith. And I desperately wanted to restore my hope. His words offered me my first glimmer of belief that not *all* hope was gone. I had so many things to be hopeful for—good health and happiness for my loved ones, my family and friends, and so on.

This would be easier said than done, at least in the beginning. It takes time, and everybody responds to loss and grief differently. Some can snap right out of it, while others, like me, just need time. There is no clock on grief. No imaginary deadline that must be met to move forward with your life.

Not long ago, I decided to pull the charm necklace Helmut had given me from my jewelry box and put it on. And when I did, I realized that necklace was the promise of three things I so desperately wanted and needed back in my life—love, joy, and hope.

Chapter Fourteen:

THE STRENGTH OF ACCEPTANCE

You may not control all the events that happen to you,
but you can decide not to be reduced by them.

—MAYA ANGELOU,

Letter to My Daughter

I am not a passive person. I am passionate. I rarely, if ever, throw my hands up and say, "Oh well," and then give up. I will always try to find my way over, under, around, or through any obstacle that comes into my path.

In 1999, I was asked to play Annie Oakley in *Annie Get Your Gun* on Broadway. Barry and Fran Weissler, two of the biggest producers in theater, called my agent, the legendary Sylvia Gold, and shared that Bernadette Peters was leaving the show in April 2000—just months away. I was thrilled at the idea. It was an absolute dream come true.

I remember going to the theater with my mother when I was younger, dreaming that someday I would be the star up there on the stage. If I said yes to the Weisslers' offer, I needed to know that I could play the part and be satisfied that I was worthy of it—not just for myself but for the company of actors I would be joining and those little girls who would be sitting in the audience dreaming their dreams too.

I discussed this opportunity with everyone who was guiding my career, from my husband to my agent. Everyone could see how excited I was about the opportunity. This was theater . . . This was BROADWAY! It's where my dreams began as a little girl. Give me an audience, and I'll entertain!

After weeks of preparation, I finally met the Weisslers and auditioned. I had worked with the two wonderful talents Marvin Hamlisch and John McDaniel to help me get ready for this meeting. After singing through a number of songs they requested, Fran and Barry Weissler told me on the spot that I got the part. We spent the next several hours talking about logistics, when Bernadette Peters was leaving the show, and what the rehearsal schedule would be like. I was exhilarated, and we hadn't even started yet! At the time, I was also filming *All My Children*, so you can imagine my schedule was already very full—and about to get fuller.

Shortly after I signed on, the producers told me that Bernadette Peters was taking a month off in December for the holidays, so they wanted me to start earlier than expected. Even though it meant I would have a much shorter time to prepare, I jumped at the opportunity. This was simply something I could not say no to. My Broadway premiere was now slated for December 23, 1999—a date that was significant for two reasons. First, it would mark my *official* Broadway debut, and second, it was my birthday.

I learned the part fast—really fast. Helmut and I went to see the show five times to get a feel for whether I could do it and to see what it was like to sit in the audience. With each show, I absorbed everything I could to help me quickly grow into the part. I continued to work with Marvin Hamlisch and John McDaniel on my singing and with my voice coach, the legendary Joan Lader.

Opening night was electric, as was every night thereafter. My parents, friends, and colleagues from *All My Children* came to cheer me on. It was very sweet to know that all of those warm and familiar faces were out there, even if I couldn't see them. Although I am shy, I am at home onstage. Still, I don't typically like to know who is in the audience until after my last curtain call. But that opening night was different because so many dear people from my life were there to support me.

After I changed out of my costume, I walked outside through the stage door with Sallie Schoneboom, my beloved publicist from ABC. We were headed to the after-party to celebrate my wonderful and unforgettable (at least to me) Broadway debut. There were police barricades everywhere, holding back the mobs. A crush of people lined the streets on both sides, and some were even standing on the tops of their cars, screaming. I turned to Sallie and said, "Did something happen? Is there a fire?"

"No, Susan. They're here for you," she said, beaming with great pride as we took in that incredible moment together. I had no idea such a thing would happen. But then again, I had been one of those fans many times, waiting to meet Sammy Davis Jr., Lola Falana, and Richard Burton. I guess I just never thought there would be those types of fans waiting for me.

I only appeared in *Annie Get Your Gun* for those four weeks, with the understanding that when Bernadette Peters left the show the following April, I would jump back into the role.

But unfortunately, that second opportunity never came to fruition. Bernadette Peters decided to extend her contract—*twice*—which was her prerogative. When she did leave the show, however, the producers of *All My Children* wouldn't let me commit to the play because they were about to embark on one of the most important storylines in the show's history—a story that would require more of my time than ever—and the material would be very intense and demanding. They simply couldn't guarantee that I would be done filming and out of the studio in time to make an eight o'clock curtain every night. Although they wouldn't tell me exactly what that story was at the time, it ended up being the story of Erica's daughter, Bianca, coming out to her.

Although I understood where the producers of *All My Children* were coming from—and I was honored to be such a central part of it—I was very disappointed about not being allowed to reprise my role as Annie Oakley on Broadway.

I *do not* take "no" easily. In fact, it was very hard for me to accept. As I said, I always find a way to make things happen.

Only this time was different.

At that moment, I didn't fully understand the demands that were going to be put on me with this new storyline. I really thought I could do both. The producers continued to assure me that, in their opinion, it couldn't be done.

I didn't know what to make of this, but finally, after *much* discussion, I accepted it. What choice did I have?

I inherently understood the very strong trust bond between myself and the producers of *All My Children*—a trust bond that time and experience had built. This was one of those occasions when I needed to rely on that trust and, despite my emotions, *accept* that they knew what was possible—and what was best for everyone.

I came to understand that acceptance is a powerful act of grace we give ourselves when life doesn't unfold as we'd hoped or expected. It's not about giving up or pretending we're unaffected—it's about embracing reality. For myself, I learned that when plans unravel, acceptance allows us to release resistance, easing the grip of frustration and disappointment. It opens a path to healing, growth, and new possibilities we might have overlooked. In accepting what is, I found strength and an ability to adapt, learning valuable lessons. I was moving forward with an open heart—or at least trying to.

Admittedly, acceptance is also sometimes hard.

When Helmut passed away, there was nothing I could do.

I spent so many sleepless nights asking myself, *Could I have done more?* Wishing I had done more. *Did I ask all the right questions? Was there something I missed?* I am sure other people who have lost their life partner and the person they love have felt this way too.

And still, once Helmut passed, there was not a thing left to do.

I had to accept that awful reality.

Although I had heard the word *acceptance* many times before, it wasn't until my husband was gone that I truly understood it.

Life keeps going on. The world keeps turning. But that first spring I couldn't understand how flowers could ever bloom again or how birds could sing. These were things I used to love, but that spring they were too painful.

The first summer without Helmut was hard. I continued to go out and be social because I knew it was good for my soul. We had spent so many of our summers in the Hamptons as a family—so many happy times. I thought it would help me feel and stay connected to him, but it just made me miss him more. Although we had sold our home there, I have a favorite little inn where I like to stay when I go out to the beach. That first summer, I spent just one week in June, July, and August at that inn. I feel at home there and well cared for by the wonderful staff.

But I'd come down in the morning and find "breakfast for one" to be a killer. As nice as everyone was, as welcoming as the place is, and as charming as the town remains, I glanced around the room each morning and saw that everyone was a couple—sometimes two couples away for the weekend with friends. *All couples.* But not me, not anymore. I had lost Helmut, my love—and I had also lost my life as I had known it.

Whether I was seated at a table for two or four, it was always just me. This was such an unfamiliar and uncomfortable feeling—one I didn't ever want to experience and one I didn't think I'd ever get used to. So I would look down at my phone and play Wordle, as people do, pretending to be busy just to hide from that feeling of being alone. It was like having an out-of-body experience. I remember thinking, *This is lame. You miss Helmut so much, you're playing Wordle at a table for one.* This wasn't working for me. Not at all.

When I got home, I decided to do something about it. I thought, *Wait a minute. I always have two cups of coffee in the morning.* When Helmut was alive, I would put out two china cups—one for Helmut and one for me—and each of us would have our two servings of coffee in our own cup. Now, I set the breakfast table for one, BUT I still put out two cups near the coffee maker. I have the first cup in my coffee cup, and the second in his. Okay, so it's still breakfast for one, but visually, it makes me feel so much better, and it still connects us in some way. Look, I get it. Everybody has to do their own thing—grieve in their own way. But I just didn't want to feel sad all the time.

Later that summer, I attended a beautiful dinner party in Washington, DC, with my college roommate and best friend, Patty Johnson, and her husband, David. It was a gorgeous garden party in the loveliest setting.

Patty put together a table for us. We were seated with their friends. I was sitting between Patty and her friend, Marjorie, who was delightful. She seemed so happy—so full of joy. In the course of our conversation, though, I learned she had recently lost her twin sister and, years before, her little daughter. As she spoke, I was taken by her warmth and fortitude.

I said to her, "You seem to be such a happy person. You're dealing with everything so well."

She looked me in the eyes, paused for just a beat, and then she spoke. "You know, at a certain point, I think it's a choice. I didn't want to be so sad all the time, so I choose not to be."

Marjorie had such a profound effect on me, lasting far beyond that evening. Her answer blew me away. I needed to figure that out because I was searching for my joy—my light. That conversation was a turning point in my grieving process. Yes, some things are a choice. We can control how we respond to almost every situation. Of course, I have learned that some things, like grief, can show up when we least expect it—when we think we are doing so well—and then the wave takes you by surprise and brings you down. But now I have made that choice. I just don't want to be sad all the time.

One thing I learned about grief is that it comes and goes. You can't schedule when it arrives or when it fades. Holidays and times of celebrations (all the "firsts") were the most difficult to navigate—they still are. I've learned to recognize what could trigger those emotions, but I can't always control when they pop up or for how long.

Throughout that first summer and beyond, amazing friends were always reaching out and inviting me to join them, especially for the holidays. I was lucky enough to be out of the country with good friends during the summer of 2023, and we celebrated the Fourth of July where we were. The following summer, I was invited to go to the Hamptons for the holiday. I knew there would be great friends to see—friends who would be fantastic and lovely—but it didn't feel right. Not then. To go to the very place where Helmut and I had spent so many summers together, so many Independence Days with these friends, and not have

Helmut with me was something I just could not do. This was two years after he passed, but it was more than I could bear, so I chose not to go.

I had been very busy with a renovation I had started on my home and used that as my excuse to decline politely. I didn't want anyone to think I wasn't okay. I was. Or at least I thought I was. But my feelings took me by surprise. I felt lost. It wasn't Helmut's birthday. It wasn't mine. It wasn't Christmas or Valentine's Day. It was the Fourth of July. I don't know why it hit me so hard—but it did.

The night before the Fourth, I reached out to a few friends, but they were busy with their families. Their grandchildren were coming over for a barbecue at their house. I then reached out to my friend, the renowned novelist Nelson DeMille, who had become the best buddy I could have ever hoped for. We were going to have dinner together anyway when he said, "Why don't you come down to my beach club. There's a terrific barbecue, and there will be fireworks tonight." I immediately agreed to go with him. And I am so glad that I did. It was a complete change of scenery and a totally different group of people, whom I knew but not as well. There was nothing there to remind me of Helmut being missing. It was a very happy atmosphere and exactly what the doctor ordered.

They say distraction is a good thing, especially when it comes to pain. I believe this is true. Nelson and I spent the evening with good friends we don't see as often, laughing and enjoying ourselves at this wonderful, real old-fashioned American barbecue on the beach.

People don't talk about how beautiful the beaches are on Long Island, but they are spectacular. They're wide and deep, and the sand is powdery and nearly white. I'm kind of glad nobody writes about them because they are gorgeous, and for the most part, we have them to ourselves. (Wait . . . did I just let the cat out of the bag? Shhh. Let's just keep this our little secret.)

Not long after that, I had dinner with two of my good friends. One had lost her husband several years before Helmut passed. And the other had lost her husband in 2024. We had so much to talk about, so much to reflect upon. We also had so many laughs. We literally closed the restaurant down as we were the last guests to leave. We all knew each other's husbands, which made our conversation easy.

Of course, we talked about the different stages of grief and how we were managing. They both talked about how they would yell at their husbands since they passed away.

"Why did you do this to me? You left me here, and now I have to deal with everything! The finances, the house—everything!" They shared this in a funny way—although I did think they were both legitimately in the anger stage of grief. They were shaking their fists in the air at their husbands for leaving them. As they were talking, I was thinking, *Gee, is something wrong with me? I don't feel that. I just don't feel it.* Aside from the initial shock and anger I felt after Helmut passed, I didn't think I had experienced any anger in the various stages of grief. And after the terrific Fourth of July barbecue and dinners like this, I was actually feeling very good. I didn't feel like I had any triggers—I thought I was progressing toward just plain happiness.

That is, until later that night.

I was lying in bed, when a video of Helmut popped up on my phone. We were at an absolutely beautiful wedding at the Plaza Hotel in New York City. The venue was filled with the most glorious flowers, and violinists were playing during the cocktail reception. Helmut, being Austrian, was so happy to be around the violinists. He looked so happy, and I was so happy to be there with him. It was a wonderful, joyous video. I could feel a warmth flow through my body as I watched. But then, a second video popped up. This one was of Helmut cooking during the COVID lockdown. There were so many snippets of him that had been compiled into this video, and I just couldn't take it. I completely broke down as if he had just passed, as if this was all brand new. I hadn't felt like this since that unforgettable and excruciating day in March 2022.

I had heard this could happen. I just never thought it would happen to me.

It had been two years and nearly four months.

I didn't expect to feel that way.

I thought I had gotten better at dealing with my grief. I knew we don't necessarily get past it, but we can get better—right?

At that moment, I wasn't angry with Helmut. It wasn't his fault he was gone. I was angry with God. Like the first time, it wasn't a long-lasting anger. I wasn't shaking my fists, but this unrecognizable sensation came over me.

I was asking God, "Why? Why did you have to take Helmut? Why did he have to have a stroke?"

The depth of grief I felt, followed by the rising anger that this had happened, took me by total surprise. It was at complete odds with how much gratitude I feel for having had Helmut in my life. Besides missing him, *that* has been the overwhelmingly constant feeling I've had—*gratitude*. Complete and utter thankfulness for his being on this planet and in my life. That is what I had been full of since he passed.

But that night, I felt this anger. Eventually, I was able to talk myself off the emotional ledge I was teetering on. I had to talk myself down. I had to allow myself to move forward. I reconciled my anger that night by focusing once again on my gratitude—because that was the truth. I know how lucky I am to have been loved like that and to have had that love in my life, and to love him in return. I know how rare that is—and I began to thank God for these blessings.

The next morning, when I awoke, I had a sense of peace. I understood that this is God's plan. As I've said, I just wished it wasn't this. But it is. And then it occurred to me, this is what people talk about when they speak of radical acceptance.

I've always loved the term *radical acceptance*, a concept that means fully accepting reality as it is, without resistance or denial, even when it's painful or difficult.

I learned that radical acceptance doesn't mean approving what happened or giving up; it's about recognizing that fighting reality, and what truly can't be changed, only intensifies suffering. I came to realize that acceptance is a gift we give to ourselves and others, opening the door to personal growth and embracing what is, so we can move forward with strength and grace.

Chapter Fifteen:

AFTER THE RAIN, THE SUN SHE SHINES

After the rain, the sun she shines.

—HELMUT HUBER,

in his adorable Austrian accent

When I was in college, my girlfriends and I would play a game. Somebody would leave the room, and when they came back, they would have to ask questions such as, "If I were a car, what kind of car would I be?" and "If I were a musical instrument, I'd be a _____." I answered I'd be a baby grand piano, given that I'm petite. On our first date, I asked Helmut if *he* were a musical instrument in an orchestra, what instrument would he be? Without batting an eyelash or taking a breath, he answered, "The conductor." Oh yeah, he made me laugh. It was such a perfect answer for him to give me and so authentic.

Helmut was infamous for his multitude of clever sayings and one-liners, often direct translations from the original German in his broken English. He was so funny, even when he didn't realize he was being funny. A couple of my favorites were, "You have to have a little fun, otherwise nobody comes to the funeral," and "After the rain, the sun she shines."

Several years ago, I had a friend whose mother-in-law had lost her husband. I always admired this woman, the way she dressed and how she always had a mix of generations around her. In my marriage, Helmut and I were very social. We were out with friends all the time, whether it was business or personal. One of the things this woman imparted to me after her husband died was that if anything ever happened, never say no to an invitation. Always say yes. Fortunately, our wonderful friends made it a point to include me after Helmut passed away, which helped me so much.

One other pearl of wisdom my friend's mother-in-law shared with me was not to make any decisions about big life changes for a year. At the time, I had never heard this advice. Of course, since then, I've heard it many times.

About six months after Helmut's funeral, I started to wonder if I was supposed to sell our house. Was I supposed to downsize? Maybe buy a condo? I considered what that might be like, so I began to explore the options. There are a few beautiful condominium buildings in my hometown, which I thought might be a possibility. I reached out to my very good friend Mary Krener, who is a real estate agent, and she took me to see one that seemed to fit what I was looking for. I came very close to making an offer, and then for one reason or another, I just thought it wasn't right.

A few months later, not long before Christmas, another condo came on the market, which Mary thought I should see. I toured the property and thought what a lovely view and beautiful terrace it had. I was leaning toward this one, but again, it didn't feel right. In the meantime, as I would pull into the driveway at my house, I would stop and think, *I love it here.* While I marveled at the view from the condo, I already had magnificent views and terraces at home. I had friends around this corner and that corner. I was comfortable and happy there. And then, Andreas told me he and his family were going to move to Miami. With that, my mind was made up. I now had an extra good reason to keep this house. Andreas came home from the hospital to this house. He loved our home, and his children loved it too. Now that they would be away, I wanted them to have this place to come back to. This was truly home, and this was where I wanted to stay.

Sometime in the early part of 2023, I thought about all the things Helmut and I had talked about doing to the house but didn't get to. I thought, *Okay, before I turn into Big Edie in* Grey Gardens, *it is time to address these renovations.* The first thing was finishing the attic.

I had never done anything like this before on my own, but I must admit, it's been a spectacular experience. In the past, Helmut had always overseen any type of building or renovation work we'd done. One thing I understood through my own experiences is the importance of being in the best hands, whether it's a physician, a director, a writer, or, yes, a general contractor.

There was a very good local contractor who worked with many people I knew. I planned to call him, but then I remembered that when we did a big renovation on our home years before, Helmut and I had worked with a wonderful contractor named Jeremy Wheaton, the owner of Hamptons Habitat. Our home in Garden City was an hour and fifteen minutes away from Westhampton, where his business is based. I wasn't sure he'd want to take on a job so far away. What I did know was that everything he did was top-tier, and he brought the most talented and engaged crew to work on our house. It gave me tremendous confidence to know that Helmut and Jeremy worked so well together. Helmut was a tough cookie, and he thought Jeremy was terrific. In fact, Jeremy and Helmut never had a harsh word between them. I also knew Jeremy had a high standard for craftsmanship and a very calm demeanor. No request was ever too much, and his crew was always beyond skilled, professional, and respectful.

When we did the first renovation and extension on our home, we didn't want it to look "new." We wanted it to look like the original house, which was built in 1927. The architect we worked with, Paul Rice, was wonderful, but the crew that Jeremy brought in was nothing short of spectacular. One day, the foreman said to me, "Mrs. Huber, I found a source for doorknobs from 1927 in Connecticut." They even found the quarry in Pennsylvania where the original slate for our roof came from. I couldn't believe the lengths they went to. They truly went above and beyond to do the job right.

I called Jeremy, who agreed to do a walk-through with me. At the end, he turned to me and said, "You know, I can feel Helmut's presence. I feel him here. He was so great to be around."

I took that as a good sign and hired him on the spot.

Originally, I thought I'd just do general repairs on the attic, but then I had an idea to turn it into the most spectacular walk-in closet. There is a store in Greenwich, Connecticut, called Richards. It was one of the few places where I could get Helmut to shop. He hated shopping. (We did not share that in common.) It is mostly a men's store, but one day while Helmut was there, the manager of the store came over to me and asked if I wanted to see something special. He pointed toward a grand staircase and said, "Would you like to take a staircase to paradise?"

If we hadn't been in a department store, I might have hesitated before I answered that question. But I knew there was something fabulous waiting for me at the top of that staircase, and I wanted to see it. So, I answered, "Sure!"

When we walked up the beautiful marble stairs, there was an entire private floor full of the best women's clothing. It was like a microcosm of Bergdorf's.

When I decided to finish the attic, I had this vision of creating a similar staircase to my own paradise. I mentioned this story to Jeremy and asked if he could make the attic a walk-in closet for me?

And, boy, did he.

Not only did he create the most beautiful closet, but he built a dressing room too. Every part I ever played, the women had the most amazing dressing rooms, with shelf lighting and dedicated space to display their treasured handbags and shoes. This had been a dream of mine for years.

As it was starting to take shape, I began working with Betty and Lisa Barbatsuly, an outstanding mother-daughter interior-design team. I had worked with Betty before, several times. I loved and trusted her taste. She has a magic touch. And Lisa's insights brought an additional take on things. Having both generations' eyes on the project made it incredibly fun and led to marvelous results.

Of course, if you've ever started a renovation of any kind, you know that one thing leads to another, and before you know it, you're redoing the bedrooms, bathrooms, kitchen, and so on. There had been closet spaces in the basement I always thought were kind of spooky. I didn't really like opening those doors because I never knew what would pop out or what we'd find. Although we had renovated the basement in the past, it also needed redoing.

I thrive on being organized. For years, I'd wanted to tackle that basement and make it very user-friendly, but I never seemed to have the time to do it. There were two other inspirations to do this. My dear friend Nelson DeMille had shared with me that he had archived his writings at Boston University. I also recalled Agnes Nixon archiving her scripts at a warehouse in Connecticut. I realized that once those spooky closets were remodeled, they might make a wonderful place to archive scripts and other memorabilia I had collected over the years. For so long, I wrote my children's menus for the day on the back of *All My Children* scripts. I'd put scripts from *All My Children*, *Devious Maids*, *Hot in Cleveland*, and so on in random drawers, and I stored sheet music from *Annie Get Your Gun*, which Marvin Hamlisch had printed out so beautifully for me, in a case on a shelf in a closet, tucked away somewhere in the abyss. These things were of great sentimental value, so I ought to have been taking better care of them.

There were also countless golf trophies from both Andreas and Helmut, awards I'd received over the years, magazines, and newspaper clippings, which are lovely to have and deserve to be on display and seen, not discarded or stored away in box after box. If not for me, then *maybe* someday for my children and grandchildren if they're interested. (Probably not, but I can dream, can't I?)

There is something so satisfying about having things the way you want them, the way they always should have been. I'm so grateful that I didn't do any of this work until now because I am choosing things that make me smile, that make me happy. There is no doubt that Helmut's vision would have been very different from what I chose to do, but that's okay. I probably would have had to get him down with a stun gun, but he would have loved the outcome. 😘

In some ways, I surprised myself by taking on such a grand project. But something extra came out of doing this on my own.

What I've learned is that I can.

Of course, I was also in such good hands. I had the chance to work with Jeremy—someone Helmut had vetted—and with his crew, who are not only craftsmen but artists for whom I have the utmost respect. In the end, I am completely over the moon with the way things have turned out.

Renovating my home has been much like starting over in life after my loss. It's been a journey of transformation built on a foundation that's weathered storms. At first, the cracks and broken pieces seemed overwhelming, just as my grief felt insurmountable. But with patience and care, walls were repaired, new colors chosen, and spaces reimagined. Every brushstroke and nail driven was an act of hope for me, a belief that beauty could rise from what felt ruined. Renovation honors the past while embracing change, much like healing after loss—proof that even after profound sadness, life can be rebuilt with strength and love.

Our homes reflect who we are. They tell a story and allow us to create the environment we are happiest in so we can thrive. When you take care of your home, it can nurture you; you are taking care of your soul. What I realized, quite unexpectedly, was I wasn't just renovating my home. I was entering into a new phase of my life—one where I would discover that, yes, I was still resilient, strong, and could still do what I set my mind to.

Chapter Sixteen:

DANCING IN LIFE'S BRIGHT MOMENTS

The purpose of life, after all, is to live it, to taste experience to the utmost, to reach out eagerly and without fear for newer and richer experience.

—ELEANOR ROOSEVELT, *You Learn by Living*

In 2015, I played a small part in the film *Joy*, written and directed by the formidable David O. Russell and starring Jennifer Lawrence as Joy Mangano. In the film, Joy is struggling financially and trying to cope with a complicated family life. She lives with her two children; her grandmother, Mimi; her wannabe singer ex-husband who sleeps in the basement; and her mother, Terri, who is addicted to soap operas and stays in bed all day. Guess what part I play? Yes, the star of the soap opera who ultimately inspires Terri to build self-confidence and take a chance on love when a surprise suitor enters her life. With time, Joy invents the Miracle Mop, an indispensable home-cleaning product, which she works so hard to get on the air. She finally sells it on QVC and becomes a self-made millionaire who sponsors other deserving inventors. The film is not only about Joy finding joy but about helping others find joy too.

After I appeared in that film, my daughter, Liza, gave me the perfect gift for my birthday, which falls two days before Christmas. It was a silver-colored metal sign with three letters that spelled out the word *Joy*. Each letter had tiny lightbulbs. With one flip of a switch, I could always find joy. And I loved it. Not because it had anything to do with me or the movie, but because it had everything to do with how lovely it was for my daughter to think of giving it to me. I keep it in the hallway off the kitchen, where I walk by it many times a day. Much to my delight, my youngest grandson loves to toggle the switch, and I love the smile that lights up his beautiful face every time he turns on the "lights of joy." Seeing him get so much pleasure out of switching on the light just fills my heart in immeasurable ways and makes me smile every time. I don't know if Liza truly knows the deep gratitude I have always felt for that gift, but it is a treasure to me.

I have often thought about the meaning of joy.

What is it?

How do I define it?

And how can I get it back?

Joy always came naturally to me, and trying to find it again is one of the driving forces in my life now. There was so much joy with Helmut. Simple things, little things, *joyful* things. And I am looking for joy again—praying for that light to come on again.

There *are* moments of joy, even now. Time spent with family, especially my grandchildren, good times with great friends and the tons of laughter we have, and the experiences of traveling and performing. These are the things that make me happy—that bring me joy.

I think keeping joy in your life requires intention. Much like choosing not to be sad all the time, joy is a choice too. It's about cultivating gratitude, keeping your heart open, and maintaining your sense of wonder, even in challenging times. It's focusing on what you have rather than what you don't have. It's learning to let your heart be light again.

So, I surrounded myself with people who uplifted me, pursued activities that ignited my passion, and reminded myself that joy isn't gone—it can come back.

After Helmut passed, I found it difficult to walk by the *Joy* sign. For a long time thereafter, my life felt joyless. Even so, I never thought about taking that sign down. It holds so much meaning for me. As it turned out, my feelings of being without joy were temporary. I learned that grieving is not linear, and it was important to give myself grace as I navigated this process. It took me a while, but one day in November

2024, having just returned from a joyous Thanksgiving with family, I realized I no longer felt sad walking past the *Joy* sign. In fact, it filled my heart in a way it hadn't for a couple of years.

Had my joy returned?

Or like my light, had it always been there?

I believe that I can find happiness again. I realize now, joyfully, that I am still becoming. I am still alive.

For me, finding joy again began with small steps. And in my case, steps past that sign every day.

I have found that time is a gentle healer when it comes to the loss of joy. In the immediate aftermath of grief, it felt impossible to imagine ever feeling light or happy again. But as days turned into weeks and months, time created space for emotions to settle and for the sharp edges of my loss to soften. It doesn't erase what happened, but it has allowed me to gain perspective, process my feelings, and begin to rebuild.

Over time, I started to notice moments of beauty or laughter creeping back into my life. These moments are growing, little by little. Time doesn't heal by itself; it's what I did with that time. First, there was acceptance—the openness I had to healing. And then, there was the active intention that gradually restored my capacity for joy.

I am not a very patient person, but I have learned how important it is to be patient. I've discovered that joy isn't about erasing the pain; it's about learning to live with it and finding new ways to experience hope and love. It takes time, but joy can and will find its way back into your life, often in the most unexpected and beautiful ways.

Chapter Seventeen:

A GOOD BOOK, LIKE A GOOD FRIEND, IS IMPORTANT TO FIND

Good books, like good friends, are few and chosen;
the more select the more enjoyable.
—BRONSON ALCOTT

I've always enjoyed reading a good book, one that shares a wonderful story and transports you to a different place and time. Among my dearest friends for many years was the wonderful and esteemed author, Nelson DeMille, who wrote *The Gold Coast*, *The General's Daughter*, and *Cathedral*, just to name a few. While it's hard for me to pick a favorite, *The Gold Coast* and *Night Fall* are two I especially love. Some of his books are set on Long Island, where I grew up and still live, which drew me to his work even more. I knew Nelson on and off for many years. Our dads knew each other. When I was a little girl, I remember my father mentioning that Nelson's uncle and his dad were builders. My father was not a builder himself, but he was in construction. As it turned out, we lived in the very neighborhood Nelson's dad and uncle built. It was amazing and ironic because many years later, Nelson had a home built in my neighborhood, very nearby.

For a while we would see each other at community events, but eventually we lost track of one another. That is, until one Saturday morning at the beach. I was at Briermere Farms picking up pies for a party Helmut and I were hosting. Briermere Farms is a farm and bakery on the North

Fork of Long Island. It has the most amazing pies, which you have to reserve to get the ones you want. The woman who was waiting on me stepped aside to bring the pies from the kitchen, still warm from the oven. As she was packing them up, I looked through the glass case and saw what looked to me like the baked apples my grandmother used to make for me as a little girl when I came home from school.

"Are those baked apples?" I asked.

"Yes, they are."

"Do you sell coffee?"

"We do!"

"I would like one of those baked apples in addition to the pies and a coffee, please." I was about to be in apple heaven.

I walked to my SUV, put the pies down on the floor of the back seat, sat in the driver's seat while parked on the dirt driveway, and opened the box with the baked apple.

Surprise!

It was much larger than it had appeared in the case.

Even better! I had no shame; I dug right in!

I was loving my baked apple with the most delicious crust while sipping on my coffee. Memories of my childhood and grandmother were rushing through my mind when suddenly I heard a *tap*, *tap*, *tap* on the window.

I looked over, and it was Nelson!

"What are you doing?" he said with a laugh.

I was so busted. I was still chewing. I'm sure I had crumbs all over my face.

I could see a very pretty blonde woman a few feet behind him, smiling like she got it. That was Sandy, his new girlfriend at the time, who turned out to be the love of his life. Nelson introduced me, and I liked her immediately. She became one of my closest friends. Nelson and Sandy married and built their beautiful home just around the corner from ours. They also had a son together, James.

I would often see Nelson at the soccer field when his son from his first marriage, Alex, and my Andreas were little boys, maybe five or six years old. We would stand on the sidelines and gravitate toward each other. We weren't running up and down alongside the soccer field screaming at our boys to run faster, kick the ball, or score a goal. We weren't caught up in the competition. We just loved watching our sons play a sport they had a good time doing.

Nelson was very generous and loved to celebrate . . . *everything*. He and Sandy would always invite people to their house for Halloween parties and pre-Thanksgiving gatherings—any reason to get a group of friends together was on the table. He and Sandy and I had that in common—we never forget to celebrate. Don't wait for a birthday, an anniversary, or a holiday. Make those connections. Somehow, Nelson inherently understood the value of those connections and friendships. I loved that so very much. Even when Sandy was diagnosed with lung cancer (she had never smoked a day in her life), we surrounded her and Nelson with our love, comfort, and support. And Nelson made sure that Sandy knew her friends were there with her.

When Sandy came home from the hospital for the last time, there was a hospice nurse with her. Nelson let us know it was time to say goodbye. There was a group of six of us who were all very close and who always had each other's backs. We wanted to be there, to tell Sandy we loved her and how much she meant to each of us. She had been an amazing mother to James, giving him so many experiences and memories to last a lifetime. She was always there for him, for Nelson, and for her friends. It was so generous of Nelson to allow us that grace to share that last time with her. And so, we did. We sat with Sandy for a while, and we held her hand, stroked her hair, and showered her with all the love we had to give. The six of us remained very good friends until Sandy passed away in 2018. And then there were five. Helmut, Nelson, and I were pretty inseparable after that. It was important for us to stay connected. It was good for Nelson and his son, James. We loved Nelson, and it was so good for all of us. Really, it was such a gift.

Sandy passed away a few years before Helmut, so Nelson understood my heartache and the journey that lay ahead for me. He was also the kind of friend who liked to be out and about—as did I—so we would go out and about together. In many ways, he became a mentor to me as well. I could talk to Nelson, and he understood how I was feeling. And in turn, he could speak openly to me too. We were always very good friends, but his losing Sandy and my losing Helmut, whom we both loved, created a bond between us that required no words. We talked often about many different topics. Our friendship was marked by tremendous mutual respect, great support for each other's careers, and many happy shared celebrations. He was such a strong influence and dear friend, and we shared a deep and enduring connection until he passed away in September 2024, just a few weeks after I hosted a birthday party for him at my home. Nelson knew that I was planning this party for him. It was a sit-down dinner that grew from sixteen to thirty-one guests. Nelson wanted all of his good friends there. And so I followed his lead with the guest list.

The sit-down dinner for thirty-one was held at a long farm table I had set out on my property to feel as if we were in Tuscany for the evening. I had always wanted to host a party like this, and doing it for Nelson was the ideal reason for it. And it turned out to be a perfect summer night.

By this time, Nelson was feeling the effects of the chemo he was undergoing more and more. Nelson would say to me, "I have chemo brain." And I would say, "Nelson, you are in *Mensa*. Your worst day of chemo fog is everyone else's best day." He would chuckle whenever I'd say that. He was fragile that night but so happy. He lit up to sit and talk with his closest friends. But then he needed to leave. He didn't make it to the dinner table. His grown son, Alex, had accompanied him to the party, so I asked Alex to slowly walk Nelson to the front door while I ran to get the caterer to light the candles on the birthday cake, and then I'd meet them as they exited the house. As Nelson stepped outside, all the guests assembled around him with the birthday cake and the lit candles, and we sang "Happy Birthday" to him. We could see that he felt our love. And even though he couldn't stay for the party, we knew how much it meant to him.

Losing Nelson wasn't easy. In this case, it was very shocking but not completely unexpected. Nelson had had a very rough year. He had been sick, battling cancer. Throughout his treatments, he remained the most amazing friend to me, but toward the end I believe he knew his time was limited. He was supposed to come to Las Vegas with a group of us but bowed out at the last minute. He wasn't up for the trip, and by that time it was very clear he wasn't able to go. But I wasn't expecting him to die when he did. Things can change in an instant. I drive by Nelson and Sandy's home every day on the way to my house. And when I do, of course, I think of them. And for a split second, my heart leaps if I see a light on and think, *Oh good, they're home.* I think of James, who holds a deep place in my heart. And I am overcome with sadness, but gratitude as well, for all of the times we shared.

I count myself very lucky that I have such good friends in my life. For many years, my career took me out of the mix a lot. At times, I would think that it must be very hard to be my friend because I wasn't always available. Of course, there are friends who have taken this ride with me for years, and I treasure them. And so many showed up for us during our time of need. I will never forget when I was in the hospital with Helmut, Mary bringing me meatballs and Sue bringing lemons for my hot water. I was so humbled and grateful for such good friends.

When I was on *All My Children*, my schedule was relentless and all encompassing. My days were filled with preparation, shooting, and getting ready for the next scene. My evenings were all about my family. My children were the focal point, and I wanted to make sure everyone was fine, safe, and loved. They were at the center of every decision I made. My husband was the other piece of that equation. I just wanted everything to be A-plus.

For years, I put my family and career over my friendships, something I don't regret, but I do wish I had been able to find a better balance back then. I didn't want any of my loved ones to suffer from the fact that I had a career, which I wanted to do well at. I think a lot of people feel like I did—as if I were shot out of a cannon with no extra space in it. The real estate of my heart, mind, eyes, and ears had no additional room to take everything in, to feel what I as a human being should feel for those beyond my inner circle. And I felt as if there was no time to do all of the things I really wanted to do. In a way, during that time, I couldn't feel the empathy for others that I felt I should have. I certainly felt everything when it came to my husband, children, and loved ones, but I felt that there were things going on in the world, stories of people I would see in the news, that I thought I should have felt more deeply for. When I didn't, I knew I was missing something—that particular type of empathy. This felt terrible. I didn't want to be like that. Somehow, it made me feel so small, as if I were less of a human being. I wanted to be a better person. I didn't intend to shut things out; I wanted to bring them in with great big open arms. I just couldn't focus on more than what was in front of me at that time.

I am one of those people who likes being busy. I have never really lounged around, doing nothing. There's always a project to be done around the house or something that needs my attention, whether it's personal, work, or family related. However, during COVID, I had a little more time than I've ever had. Now that I am not on a series or being pulled in so many different directions, I can feel that I have developed my empathy. I am so grateful to have those feelings, especially with the horrific things going on in the world today. I can't speak for anyone except myself, but I think there is so much noise in the world making us numb. We feel nothing when we need to be feeling something for others who are hurting, suffering, or grieving, or who have lost everything. Now, I must say, I do. Without question, I do.

After I became a drama major in college, I remember the head of the department walking onto the stage one day and saying he would be imitating someone in the class. He did this often, but on this particular day, he took the stage in a very poised manner, bearing a great big smile. Well, I immediately realized that he was imitating me. It was both embarrassing and hysterically funny. It was also a revelation. While this might sound harsh, his point was well taken. I think this may have been the first time I began thinking about the difference between how you really feel, as opposed to how you present yourself. Look, it's not always appropriate to present yourself the way you really feel. As an actress, I learned to compartmentalize the two.

About a year before Helmut died, one of Andreas's closest friends from college lost his father. His mother was French and his father American. The father and son were very good golfers and athletes. Helmut and I loved Andreas's friend, Tristan. His parents had become friends of ours and had been to our home many times.

When Tristan's father died, I reached out to Tristan but not his mother, Patricia. I had intended to. I thought about it—many times—but I never did. That is, until one of the days when I was in the hospital with Helmut after his stroke. It was pretty clear that Helmut wasn't going to make it. Something propelled me to finally text Tristan's mother. I hadn't understood what she and her family had gone through until I found myself on the verge of losing Helmut. Then, I got it. Big time. I was ashamed of myself. I had to own my mistake—my absence as her friend when she needed it. When I reached out, I wrote, "I am so sorry. I am sorry I wasn't there for you more. I didn't get it, and I am ashamed of myself. I apologize, and I am so sorry for your loss."

I felt compelled to let her know how badly I felt for not being a better friend. I needed to cleanse this. A year had gone by, and I really didn't think she would answer. In fact, I thought she might tell me to go to hell. I would have completely understood if she had. But she didn't. Instead, she answered me with grace and magnanimous, kind, appreciative words. She also sent me a book called *Healing After Loss: Daily Meditations for Working Through Grief* by Martha W. Hickman, which became one of the most important and helpful resources in my journey after losing Helmut. It is dog-eared and marked up from reading it and rereading it for the first couple of years after Helmut died.

I took a risk that day to send the text and express what was coming from my heart. I also allowed myself to be vulnerable in the face of taking that risk. I was certainly in a very vulnerable place. I was also in a place where I realized—perhaps for the first time—what it felt like for so many others who had endured this type of loss. I grew up in a generation of women who were taught to be polished and poised and not to share their innermost vulnerability. But not anymore, not now—we all have experiences as we go along in life, and hopefully, we learn from them. I learned a lot from Patricia's generosity and from owning my own shortcomings.

The only thing I know that stays the same in life is change. So, I want to embrace life, as both Nelson and Helmut did. Enjoy every moment—celebrate the moments—big and small. One of my favorite moments was being a passenger in the car when Helmut was driving—whether we were going to the beach; to QVC in Pennsylvania for an appearance promoting my beauty line; to the Adirondacks to visit our friends, Marylou Whitney and her husband, John Hendrickson; to stay at the Lake Placid Lodge; or to take a drive in the country, going nowhere in particular. It didn't matter if it was for business or pleasure because it was a pleasure being in the car with him. Sometimes, I would look over and stare at the traces of his dimples or look into his twinkling blue-green eyes that so reminded me of a lion's eyes. They were very similar in shape. I spent a lot of time taking in my husband's profile from the passenger seat of our car. I would tell him that I wanted him to know how much I loved him and how handsome he was. I think it's so important to let your true feelings out. What's the good of keeping it in? Let that person know how you feel!

For as long as I can recall, I always thought Helmut and I would go together. We were traveling so much, flying constantly. And I may have mentioned that Helmut loved to drive fast. I was never afraid with him behind the wheel. I knew he was an excellent driver and someone who was always in command and control. We took many long drives together, but one of my absolute favorites was driving back from Atlanta after the first season of filming *Devious Maids*. We drove through the Shenandoah Valley in April. It was so beautiful! The greenest grass coming alive in the springtime, and flowers, dogwoods, and azaleas were scattered throughout the rolling hillsides. It was spectacular. I can truly understand why people who are from that part of the country have such a deep feeling for it. We stopped at the Inn at Little Washington one night, which lived up to its stellar reputation. It is an internationally renowned luxury hotel and restaurant located in Washington, Virginia, about seventy miles southwest of Washington, DC. It is known for its world-class dining and impeccable hospitality and has earned three Michelin stars, the highest distinction in the culinary world. It was the first and only restaurant in the Washington, DC, area to receive this honor. And for Helmut, who was a classically trained chef, it was divine to experience such culinary creativity and greatness. We had always wanted to go there, and on that trip driving back to New York from Atlanta, we did.

Of course, driving in the Austrian Alps with Helmut was always a great adventure too. One day, as he drove along a very narrow mountain road—with a cast on his leg—Helmut pointed out a series of small huts that dotted the hillside. He said, "See those little huts all the way up the mountain? That's where the farmers make fresh cheese, which they bring down the mountain and sell to the townspeople and restaurants in the surrounding little villages."

The cows that lived up in the mountains looked different from the cows I was used to seeing in America. They looked prehistoric. "Have these cows ever had their hooves on level ground?" I wondered.

After all, they had lived their entire lives in the Austrian Alps! Of course, Helmut let out a hearty laugh and then punched the accelerator and drove us to the next village, where we stopped for lunch. It was just the two of us on that trip, which was rare. We both ordered pasta, and of course, the waiter asked if we would like some cheese. Helmut turned to me and said, "This is the place to have the cheese, it came from right up there on the mountain." He was right! It was the best cheese.

There were so many days and nights when I'd think of these memories, and I'd be in tears missing my husband so much—missing those wonderful times with him. Now, as I share these stories with you, I'm in a place where, whenever I think of these things, they make me smile.

So, given Helmut's love of driving fast, if I ever thought about death and dying, it always involved the two of us passing together. I would have preferred that. That way, neither of us would have had to endure the excruciating grief. I also knew if I went first, I was going to have to watch him with some other woman, and that was going to drive me crazy. I was not going to be magnanimous. I would have been finding a way to throw my stilettos down at him from heaven. (Okay, while I have never actually thrown a stiletto at him, I have learned along the way that throwing something flimsy like a bathrobe gives you no satisfaction at all.)

Erica Kane had lots of chances to throw things. I will never forget the infamous food fight with Adam Chandler right after room service delivered biscuits, caviar, champagne, fruit, and nuts. Erica was expecting Jackson Montgomery to show up at her hotel room. When she answered, it was Adam standing there. He was definitely not welcome. Erica threw everything on that service cart at him to let him know she was NOT happy to see him.

After Helmut passed, it didn't take long before I decided I wanted to know everything I could discover about the afterlife. Could it be? Was it possible? *Signs* by Laura Lynne Jackson was the first book I read on this topic. It was sent to me by a good friend, and how I discovered there are signs all around us—and they are real. Before reading this book, I was not aware that signs from the afterlife existed. However, I was interested to learn from her writing that dimes are often a sign from a loved one. I hadn't realized it at the time, but after Dany and Mirella went back to Europe following Helmut's funeral, I walked into the bedroom where they had stayed in our home, and I spotted something on one of the bedside tables. I couldn't believe my eyes. It was a ziplock bag filled with dimes! Now, this was perhaps a week or so after they left, and I had just read *Signs*. From that day on, I have continued to find dimes in the most unexpected places. And it makes so much sense as Helmut's birthday was October 10 (10/10).

And then came feathers.

I started to find feathers everywhere—in my home, outside my home, and even during my travels to Europe. During one trip to Paris, I was going to the exquisite Le Jules Verne restaurant, located in the Eiffel Tower, with close friends. As we headed to the elevator to go up the tower, I saw a feather right in front of my foot. Our dear friends were aware that Helmut sends me feathers, and we were all absolutely stunned but not entirely surprised to see one that night. There were no other feathers around except right where my food was about to land. It was magical.

However, one of the most endearing and touching and astonishing moments came from my grandson, Wolf, who was six years old at the time. Wolf and his sister, Valentina, were spending the morning with me. We were playing outside. When it came time to leave, I bent down to give Wolf a hug. Just then, he took his hand from behind his back, held up a single feather, and said, "This is for you, Lola." It took my breath away. He could have handed me a flower, a leaf, or nothing at all. But he didn't. He handed me a feather.

Intrigued, I next came across another powerful book, *Proof of Heaven: A Neurosurgeon's Journey into the Afterlife* by Eben Alexander. Reading this book changed my life. And it strengthened my faith. Dr. Alexander was a skeptic. A man of science, who believed these experiences were nothing but fantasy until it happened to him. Was that a coincidence? I don't think so. I believe it was part of the divine plan. Without his story, his belief, his willingness to change his perspective, none of us would be able to embrace the lessons he shares or the beauty in the outcome of his story.

I also read the incredible book *On Death and Dying* by Elisabeth

Kübler-Ross, an esteemed doctor and author I greatly admire. She spent her entire career caring for the terminally ill, from little children to aged adults. This book grew out of one of the most important psychological studies of the late twentieth century: Dr. Kübler-Ross's famous interdisciplinary seminar on death, life, and transition. In this remarkable work, Dr. Kübler-Ross explores what she refers to as the five stages of death: denial and isolation, anger, bargaining, depression, and acceptance. I definitely needed to learn more about that.

When I wasn't reading, I listened to podcasts, TED Talks, whatever I could find that would offer some comfort, direction, and advice. For a while, I listened to David Kessler talk about what he called the six elements of good grief on YouTube.[7] As he spoke, I found myself vigorously jotting down notes, hanging on to his every word. Here's what I wrote down:

1. Surround yourself with community.
2. Love never dies—we continue the connection with loved ones.
3. Your grief does not define you—honor your grief but don't lose yourself.
4. Treat yourself with kindness, be your own best friend, don't rush.
5. Don't compare others' opinions. They don't matter. Be gentle with yourself.
6. Count your wins—you can put one foot in front of the other, and you're standing up and not lying in a puddle on the floor.

I've kept those notes on my nightstand as a reminder ever since I heard him speak. Believe me, there are still days I need to remind myself.

I have found, in life's most challenging moments, it is the comforting presence of good friends and good books that becomes a lifeline. Friends have a warmth of understanding, the steadying hand of encouragement that we are not alone. Our laughter together can brighten the darkest days, and their compassion helps in every way. Meanwhile, books open doors to worlds beyond our own, offering wisdom, solace, and an escape. Together, friends and books create a sanctuary—a place where we can rest and heal.

These are some of the books that I read and reread and that gave me comfort and helped me—first to get up off the floor and then to move forward.

SUSAN'S READING LIST

1. *Healing After Loss: Daily Meditations for Working Through Grief* by Martha W. Hickman
2. *When You're Ready, Written for KinderMourn* by Rob Healy (Sent to me by his dad, Bob Healy, whom I went to high school with.)
3. *Touching Two Worlds: A Guide for Finding Hope in the Landscape of Loss* by Sherry Walling
4. *Sunrise Gratitude: 365 Morning Meditations for Joyful Days All Year Long* by Emily Silva
5. *Moonlight Gratitude: 365 Nighttime Meditations for Deep Tranquil Sleep All Year Long* by Emily Silva
6. *In My Time of Dying: How I Came Face-to-Face with the Idea of an Afterlife* by Sebastian Junger
7. *Build the Life You Want: The Art and Science of Getting Happier* by Arthur C. Brooks and Oprah Winfrey
8. *More Beautiful than Before: How Suffering Transforms Us* by Steve Leder
9. *Signs: The Secret Language of the Universe* by Laura Lynne Jackson
10. *Proof of Heaven: A Neurosurgeon's Journey into the Afterlife* by Eben Alexander

11. *On Death and Dying: What the Dying Have to Teach Doctors, Nurses, Clergy and Their Own Families* by Elisabeth Kübler-Ross
12. *On Grief and Grieving: Finding the Meaning of Grief Through the Five Stages of Loss* by Elisabeth Kübler-Ross and David Kessler
13. *On Life after Death* by Elisabeth Kübler-Ross

Chapter Eighteen:
THE IMPORTANCE OF PLAY

It is a happy talent to know how to play.

—RALPH WALDO EMERSON

I feel so lucky to be in a profession that not only allows for play—but play is actually essential to it!

To begin with, I had the time of my life playing Erica Kane and so many other characters that followed. In retrospect, I've been playing since I used to dress up with items from my mother's closet. You might say play has been a part of my life since my earliest days—and not just mine. I remember seeing dancers on the street in the theater district and Central Park during the COVID lockdown. Musicians held jam sessions in their basements, and singers sang from the balconies of their apartment buildings. And then there was me, just needing to put on my gowns and run outside to twirl, skip, and play on our lawn in them. Doing this was magical. It made me feel free and like me. For people who are performing artists, we just have to do what we have to do. That's how I felt. And I am sure that is how these other performers felt too. How lucky we all are to have that outlet. I'm not sure what a brain surgeon does for play—perhaps a round of golf—but I'm pretty sure they are not twirling in a gown in the operating room. At least I hope not.

In 1990, I was cast in the television film *The Bride in Black*, directed by James Goldstone. I played Rose D'Amore, a woman who works in a Brooklyn Italian deli. Rose marries the outgoing and handsome Owen Malloy, played by David Soul, but tragically, Owen is fatally shot on their wedding day as they exit the church. Determined to uncover the truth about her husband's mysterious past, Rose embarks on a journey that reveals Owen's true identity as Johnny McGuire, a boxer and art forger involved in creating counterfeit Greek art.

We filmed *The Bride in Black* in Pittsburgh. For two weeks during rehearsals, I'd go to a local deli owned by an Italian family and learn how to make mozzarella cheese and bocconcini. In the opening scene, I am actually making fresh mozzarella!

It was such a great experience, especially since I'm half Italian. I remember thinking, *Now I can pass this on to my daughter, and make these recipes a generational thing.*

Did I do that?

Regretfully, no.

By the time we finished filming, I had completely forgotten how to make bocconcini. And buying fresh mozzarella at a great Italian deli was a lot easier than making it! Even so, at the time, I loved learning this.

Besides, by the second week of rehearsals, I had started taking boxing lessons for the role too. While it had never been on my list of things to do, I was game when I found out I'd have to box in the movie. Besides, I thought it would be fun to learn something new. And it was. I loved every minute of it.

Danny Aiello III was the stunt coordinator on the film and had been a boxer himself. What an opportunity to learn boxing from him! He had me training with a heavy bag and a jump rope; then we'd spar in the ring. This was the real deal. I wasn't a boxer, but I had some background as a dancer, which helped with my movements. There was also a certain amount of choreography too. It was inspiring, and after a few weeks of lessons, I gained a great deal of admiration and respect for the endurance and coordination it takes to become good. I had the best time. And Danny told me I had a great right hook!

Sometimes I'd work all day and night and find myself jumping rope and rehearsing at two in the morning. I didn't care. I was having a great time. It felt more like play than work.

Throwing punches at my trainer took a little getting used to, but there was more to come. After my tenth Emmy nomination and loss, I did a sugar substitute commercial that required me to slap one of the men. After several takes, the director said to me, "I want you to actually slap him."

As I'm sure you can imagine, this wasn't something I wanted to do. Sure, my character Erica had slapped her fair share of people throughout the years, but there is an art to an on-camera slap where you set the shot with the cameraman and director and "hit" at an angle without actually making contact with the other person.

When I first got the role for Erica, my mother, who was a nurse, always said not to slap anybody because you can break the blood vessels in their face. "And by all means, Susan, don't ever let anyone slap you!"

I stood there on the stage in front of this very handsome actor and asked, "Are you okay with the direction?"

"Sure," he said with a smile.

"Really?" I asked him.

Well, I wound up doing several takes in which I slapped him quite a few times. The tagline for the commercial was, "What does a person have to do around here to win an Emmy?" (Which was something I ad-libbed for the commercial, and they loved it so much they kept it.)

Of course, it was all in the name of fun. And while I had no reason to believe I would actually win the Emmy the following year, that's eventually what happened. I wound up shooting three extra versions so they could continue to run the commercial just in case I didn't win that year . . . or the next year . . . or the year after that. In fact, I didn't win the Emmy for six more years! We didn't plan *that* far in advance!

It's funny how we end up doing things we never thought we'd do. Learning new skills to play a part well has always been so fulfilling. Especially when they are physical skills. Actually, I always love to learn new skills anywhere I can.

My son is a wonderful golfer. He began playing as a little boy at eight years old. By the time he was twelve, he had done so well in junior sports programs, he was asked to be on the varsity high school golf team.

When I wasn't working, I loved driving Andreas and his friends to golf matches. For one thing, it was great listening to them talking in the back of the SUV. They were always so full of banter—so funny. One day, after the boys had won their match, I picked them up and took them back to our golf club. Despite having just finished a round of golf, they wanted to play another eighteen holes before dark. I sat on the split-rail fence right outside the men's grill at the club and watched my son tee off.

Out of the blue, Andreas turned around and called out to me, "Mom, come up here and hit one."

This was the first tee, directly in front of the clubhouse where everyone can watch you hit the ball. I was naturally—and for good reason—reluctant. I am not a golfer. And, besides, I was wearing a sundress, a straw hat, and wedges. I was hardly dressed for golf. Polo, maybe—if I were watching, not riding—but golf? No. I'd make a complete fool of myself.

Everything inside of me was shouting, "No way!" But I could see Andreas really wanted me to do it. So, what else could I say, except okay?!

As mentioned, I didn't play golf at all. I had been to the driving range with my dad many times as a teenager because he was an avid golfer. But that wasn't enough to expect I'd be any good.

As I walked toward Andreas, I was praying to the golf gods, *Please let me remember how to hold the club, and please, at least let me make contact with the ball.*

By this time, all the guys from the men's grill came out, standing with their arms folded, watching. I could almost hear them thinking, *Oh yeah. This is going to be good. We can't wait to see this.*

I took the club in my left hand, placed my right pinkie over my left forefinger and gripped the club as my father had taught me. I widened my stance, took a deep breath, swung the club back, and then, *thwack!* I hit the ball!

I made contact and it wasn't bad. In fact, not bad at all. Andreas called out, "Good shot, Mom!"

Oh, that was music to my ears—even the guys who came outside to watch were giving me a little round of applause.

As for me? Well, I was so relieved I hadn't made a complete fool of myself.

After that, I took a lesson or two with a golf pro, and I really enjoyed it. And I wasn't terrible. I truly love being in nature, and most golf courses are quite beautiful and peaceful. There is something about golf that forces you to be present in the moment, which appeals to me as well.

I think it's important to remember the value of *playing*. As the saying goes, "All work and no play makes Jack a dull boy." Or as I like to say . . . "All work and no play makes Susan a cranky, over-caffeinated woman who deserves a vacation and a glass of champagne—immediately."

Chapter Nineteen:
THANK YOU FOR ASKING

It's better to be happy than well dressed.

—IRIS APFEL

For as long as I can recall, whenever I do an interview, there are two questions I am asked more than any other. First, "Who was the best kisser?" Of course, I would never answer that question! Well, maybe in my next book. Second, I am frequently asked how I felt not to win the Emmy all those years? That's easy! Not great. After my ninth year of not hearing my name called for Best Actress, I pretty much stopped hearing the name that was called when the envelope was opened. For a split second, my hearing went numb. I listened, but I didn't hear. I was always happy for my colleagues, who were also doing wonderful work, but I think it was more of a self-protective reaction so I wouldn't feel bad or get my hopes up too much. Despite any rumors to the contrary, there were never any behind-the-scenes meltdowns after the show or moments of breaking things because I hadn't been awarded the Emmy. How could there be when I knew my children were waiting for me at home with lots of hugs and kisses, precious homemade signs, balloons, handwritten notes, poems, and freshly baked chocolate cake?! Any one of these was more valuable than that elusive Emmy!

Having said that, winning felt pretty darn good—winning is definitely better!

These days, there is one other question that comes up almost every time.

"Is there anything that people don't know about you?"

The quick answer is YES! Lots of things.

But maybe after reading this book, you might know more about me than you ever wanted to!

When that question is asked, in the moment, I can never think of anything all that interesting; however, sometime after I leave the interview, I think to myself, *Why didn't I say this?* (And I do answer it in the first question below!)

In my first book, I had a chapter called "My Favorite Things." Happily, readers loved it. It was just a list of some of my favorites—from my skin-care regimen to the music I love—but it resonated with readers, so I thought it might be fun to do something like that again for this book. This time, along with some of my favorite things, I am answering some of the most frequently asked questions I receive via social media or during appearances and interviews.

I may have also been inspired by the *Vogue* "73 Questions" videos, which I personally love to watch. Bad Bunny, Anna Wintour, Dua Lipa, Nicki Minaj, Gwyneth Paltrow, Jennifer Lopez, Lizzo, Olivia Rodrigo, and countless others have participated with *Vogue*, answering a series of seventy-three rapid-fire questions.

Here's a fun idea—you can answer these questions for yourself too or get to know someone else by asking them these questions. They're great icebreakers—fun, funny, and informative!

So here we go, and . . .

Thank you for asking!

1. WHAT'S SOMETHING NO ONE KNOWS ABOUT YOU?

I had a friend in second grade by the name of Maribel McSherry. After school, I would sometimes go to her house. She had an older sister, and the three of us would sit in front of her black-and-white television and watch *American Bandstand.* I was seven years old, thinking, *This is so much fun.* A couple of years later, we gathered to watch *The Mickey Mouse Club*, which usually came on around the time our mothers were preparing dinner. Maribel and I loved watching the show. One day—I think we were around eleven years old—we each decided to write a letter to *The Mickey Mouse Club*. Our logic was simple: They didn't have a Maribel or a Susan. In my letter, I explained I could sing and dance and often performed around my house and at birthday parties. I thought surely that would get their attention. We both assumed if we wrote a letter, they'd put us in the club. We never got a response. In retrospect, I'm not sure that any of our reasons were very impressive. I suppose this was my first official rejection! Of course, I ended up working at ABC, which was acquired by Disney during my years on *All My Children*, where I actually did have the chance to meet Mickey Mouse. When I said hello, all I could think was, *Was it you, Mickey? Did you reject me?* as we stood together for a photo.

2. IF YOU COULD HAVE A DINNER PARTY WITH ANYONE, WHO WOULD YOU INVITE AND WHY?

This question is always a struggle because when you're hosting a dinner, it's a challenge to put the right mix of people together who have something to say to each other and who bring something wonderful to the table. That said, my first choice would be Chef José Andrés of World Central Kitchen. Of course, he does such important, valuable, wonderful work feeding people around the world, but he also has this great, big, fabulous personality. I first saw José Andrés in action on the CNN show *Searching for Spain*. He was so full of warmth, charm, and charisma. As he toured Spain, he showed his two grown daughters his country and culture through food. What a great way to become acquainted with your family heritage and to witness the relationships your dad has with his colleagues. And he can cook too! Okay, so maybe I have a thing for chefs with big personalities.

Another wonderful addition to this dinner party would have to be Snoop Dogg. I don't know Snoop, but I have come to love him after watching the 2024 Summer Olympics and *The Voice*. I just love his sense of humor, his incredible warmth, his big heart, and how beautifully he speaks to the singers he judges and mentors. He treats them with such respect and is genuinely touched by their talent. He is so full of humanity, and I know he would be fun at a party!

And speaking of fun, I would include Mick Jagger at this dinner too. I've never met him, but I've always been a fan. If you were to ask me to pick between the Beatles and the Stones, it is always the Rolling Stones! I love his audacious, bodacious performances, yet at the same time, he seems so authentic. (This is true for all of my guests.) And especially true for Elton John, whom I would have to add to the mix.

I would also love to include Celine Dion at this epic dinner. While I don't know her well, Celine and her husband, René Angélil, were always very gracious to Helmut and me. The first time Helmut and I saw her in concert in Las Vegas, the show was totally sold out; however, René offered us his seats. That was the first time I met Celine, who would later make an appearance on *All My Children* in 2007 when she performed her hit song "That's the Way It Is" during her scene. She was so much fun and so great to talk to. And like most of the world, I watched Celine come back after a long health battle when she sang triumphantly in Paris during the opening ceremony of the Summer Olympic Games.

In addition, I would love to have James Bond at this dinner. Not an actor playing James Bond, but the actual Bond . . . James Bond. He's handsome, worldly, funny, drives fast cars . . . he's right up my alley! In the absence of the real James Bond, however, Sean Connery, Pierce Brosnan, and Idris Elba would always be invited!

And just for fun, let's add Javier Bardem, Bradley Cooper, David Beckham, and the world-champion rugby team! I say this because one day I found myself mysteriously mesmerized by watching the world rugby playoffs and thinking, *Now these are some strong and good-looking guys!*

3. WHERE IS THE STRANGEST PLACE YOU'VE BEEN ASKED FOR A PHOTO/AUTOGRAPH?

People approach me in the ladies' room (you know who you are) more than you might imagine. These encounters are always a little awkward because, well, I'm in the ladies' room! It might happen with a group of women who are on a girls' trip or with someone who recognizes me. I usually suggest we step outside, but they don't seem to care. They'll say, "No, here is fine. We can take the photo here." So, I do, though I try not to have a stall in the background!

One time I ran into some women who I realized were a group of backup singers for Chaka Khan. When I walked into the bathroom, Chaka Khan saw me in the mirror, turned around, and threw her arms around me. I threw mine around her, and then we grabbed hands. We were jumping up and down at the thrill of meeting each other. It was like seeing an old friend. She was so warm and kind. And then, her backup singers joined in too! It must have been very funny for anybody else coming into the ladies' room to see that.

4. WHAT IS YOUR SECRET TO GIFT GIVING?

I think the secret to being a good gift giver is to keep your eyes and ears open. If it's for one of your children or your spouse, just listen as you go along during the year. In the course of conversation, they might say something that will clue you in.

5. WHAT IS THE MOST EPIC GIFT YOU'VE EVER RECEIVED?

Helmut was so clever, especially when it came to gift giving. I told him once that I would love a strand of pearls. Well, this was many years ago, so when I mentioned it to Helmut, he said, "You're too young for pearls. Pearls remind me of my mother!" I didn't agree. But he said no. He dismissed the idea as if it were the worst thing I'd ever mentioned. A few months later, on Valentine's Day, he and I were having breakfast at our kitchen table. Suddenly, he reached under the table and brought out a double-strand, opera-length pearl necklace with a diamond clasp. Needless to say, I gasped and threw my arms around him. I absolutely loved it. He was really good at setting me up to think I wasn't getting something, and then he always came through. And then, sometime not long after that, an artist came to paint a mural that started in our foyer and continued up the stairs. The artist and I were looking through some books for ideas when we came upon a tonal, classic mural we both knew was the right feel for the foyer. We were so excited, we actually joined hands and jumped up and down. (I guess I do that when I am excited! First, Chaka Khan and then this artist!) We now knew the way we were going, and it couldn't have been better. Something reminded me of that Valentine's Day Helmut gave me the pearls, so I shared the story with her, which she loved. Unbeknownst to me, she took it upon herself to paint a bird in flight with a double strand of pearls. It was so personal and very meaningful to Helmut and me. It gave our home an even more personal feeling.

6. HAVE YOU EVER DEALT WITH A TABLOID SCANDAL?

Yes, I have, but it was relatively minor. I was walking through an airport several years ago and saw a tabloid on the newsstand. On the cover was a picture of me leaning against Anthony Geary's cheek. Tony played Luke on *General Hospital*. At the time, I had never even met Tony. I knew who he was, and that he is a wonderful actor, but I didn't know him. It was crazy to see this! I felt compelled to tell the people I was with, "This never happened!" This was well before the days of cameras on phones and social media, but clearly not before Photoshop!

7. WHAT IS YOUR FAVORITE MONTH?

I love December. It's my birthday month; my first grandchild was born on my birthday in December (as I wrote about in my first book); and of course, it's the holidays. It's such a festive and happy time of the year. If I had to pick a runner-up, I'd pick June, which reminds me of my childhood, getting out of school for the summer and enjoying the perfect weather!

8. WHAT'S A FUNNY STORY NO ONE KNOWS?

Our family had a dog named Oscar for fifteen years. At first, we were going to name him Emmy so I could have at least one. But Helmut said, "Forget Emmy. Let's go for the big one and name him Oscar!" He was a wonderful dog who just wanted to be near you all the time. When I came home at night, he would immediately lie down so I could rub his belly. I'd say, "You're such a slut, Oscar." Well, little did I know how right that was. On one night in particular, Oscar sneaked out of the house and went missing. Helmut, the children, and I were so upset. We looked for him everywhere, even in neighboring towns. We called the police department and the fire department. Our friends got on bikes, but we could not find Oscar. The next morning, I was making coffee in the kitchen, and I thought I saw something walking past the front windows. I followed that motion, ran to the front door, opened it, and found Oscar. He was filthy and had a great big smile on his face! I am not really sure exactly where he went, but I do know he was madly in love with Charcoal, the female dog across the street!

9. WHOSE HAND TURNS THE PAGES OF THE BOOK IN THE ORIGINAL OPENING OF *ALL MY CHILDREN*?

In January 2025, I attended a reunion celebrating fifty-five years of the *All My Children* debut. (The show was on the air for forty-one years.) Beloved head writer Lorraine Broderick shared something I had never known until that day. It is the hand of Agnes Nixon! I always thought it was Mary Fickett, the lead actress playing Ruth Brent when the show made its debut. This information made my heart smile. And it feels so right to know it is Agnes's hand.

10. WHAT WAS YOUR FAVORITE TIME PERIOD ON *ALL MY CHILDREN*?

Hands down, it was when Erica was in New York modeling. I photograph taller than I am, so this was my only chance for a modeling career. I'm five two on a good day, but what fun we had! We shot on location all over New York City. A favorite location was the Metropolitan Museum of Art—home of the now-famous Met Gala, but years before! It was the era of the supermodel, and I got to be one for a time. We filmed a particularly memorable scene there that involved me wearing a gorgeous white jersey gown, a matching white stole, and of course, very high heels. The hair and makeup for these scenes were extraordinary and so much fun for all of us. I had never seen such glamour and high fashion on television. I loved every single look they created for Erica. When it came time to do this scene, the producer Jackie Babin and I were standing at the top of the grand staircase, off to the side. She told me she wanted me to walk to the center at the top of the staircase, turn to the front and pause, spread my arms out so that the stole would show, and then run down the center of the staircase. Now, if you've never been to the Met, this staircase is stone, steep, and very long. And holding on to railings was not a part of her vision for this very dramatic scene. She simply asked me to do this, and I said, "Okay." I just went all in and did it! In heels. And a long gown! And it was fabulous! Thank goodness it worked on the first take!

11. I AM OFTEN ASKED, "DO YOU EAT?"

The answer may surprise you, but I never want to miss a meal! Really. Just ask anyone who was in hair and makeup with me in the morning. They will tell you I have a good appetite. In fact, some may even say, "She eats like a truck driver."

And they would be right. I was the first to instigate ordering in for lunch. Okay, so as long as we are on the topic, you may be asking, "What do you eat?" I'll go there. I eat much differently now than I did in my early days at *All My Children*. I was so surprised, but when I started doing Pilates in 1995, I no longer craved cheeseburgers, tacos, or even—and I still can't believe this—french fries. So, while I am very health conscious, eating lots of blueberries, salmon, and salads, I still occasionally crave spaghetti and meatballs, and I give in to that craving. Lucky for me, I don't have a sweet tooth, but I have a secret love affair with bread and a bowl of mashed potatoes! Having said that, I do love ice cream. I would eat ice cream on cardboard. A newish discovery for me—and I will pass it on to you in case you are watching calories too—is Yasso's chocolate-covered frozen-yogurt bites called Poppables. These look like the bonbons you get at the movie theater, and they're only thirty-five calories!

12. WHAT'S YOUR GUILTY PLEASURE?

One is watching QVC and HSN and ordering things—*some* I don't even need. For example, I ordered not one but two biscuit-making kits because I suppose I thought it would be great to have one at my home and one out at the beach. I just wanted to make biscuits everywhere! (See? I really do like bread . . . and biscuits!) Turns out, making biscuits is hard. We have such a good bakery in town that makes biscuits I actually love. And, well, it is just easier to buy them. I'm not even sure where those biscuit-making kits are anymore.

My other guilty pleasure has been taking a bubble bath . . . wait for it . . . while eating Hershey's Kisses. Yes, I said it. So, see question eleven, and add this to the list too!

13. WHAT'S YOUR BEST ADVICE TO WOMEN ABOUT MEN?

I've never been one to give advice, but for me, I love a smart, strong man taking charge. When a stupid man takes charge, it's a pain in the neck! Also, run away as fast as you can from a phony—don't walk. Run.

14. DO YOU HAVE YOUR OWN BARBIE?

While I personally don't have my own Barbie, I am thrilled to admit that I have two Erica Kane Barbie dolls. One is a bride; the other is in a white gown. To be honest, I feel the dolls could have been better reflections of Erica. For example, both dolls are in white, something I wouldn't have done. Of course, the bride in white makes sense, but I would have preferred to see the second Erica Barbie in a red gown, as this was Erica's signature color. When the artist came to measure me for the dolls, he never once looked me in the eyes. He was all about his measuring tape and not about looking at the person he was going to be creating a doll for. I kept trying to catch his eye, but he never made eye contact with me. He measured the space between my nostrils, the distance between my eyes, and the length of my eyebrows. He stood so close to me, and yet, he never locked eyes.

On the contrary, the porcelain doll that was sold on HSN was a Susan Lucci doll. That doll was done with such great care and a great eye.

Finally, there is the Erica Kane wax figure at Madame Tussauds in New York. That was done with such precision. They sent a team of artisans—among them was one to match my skin color. She had an artist's easel with her so that she could mix and match hues until she got the perfect skin tone. Someone came with a tray of eyeballs. Another with a tray of teeth. They held these things up to me in a rehearsal hall at the ABC studio, full of natural light, until they got everything exactly right. I stood on a revolving platform while they moved me in increments of an inch at a time, photographing me from every angle. That process took well over an hour—maybe even two—while I struck a pose and held it for the entire time.

Rapid-Fire Round

WHAT'S YOUR FAVORITE ANIMAL?

A dog

WHAT DO YOU HATE HEARING?

"Goodbye"

WHAT WORD DO YOU HAVE A HARD TIME PRONOUNCING?

Supercalifragilisticexpialidocious

WHAT IS YOUR FAVORITE SEASON?

Spring

WHAT IS YOUR FAVORITE SHOE?

Stilettos—high heels—the higher the better.

WHAT'S YOUR GO-TO COMFORT FOOD?

Pasta

WHAT'S YOUR FAVORITE DESSERT?

Ice cream—two words that don't even begin to say how much I love ice cream. Have I mentioned I love ice cream?

WHAT'S YOUR FAVORITE FLAVOR OF ICE CREAM?

I love pistachio and vanilla—especially vanilla at Cipriani's

IF YOU HADN'T BECOME AN ACTRESS, WHAT WOULD YOU BE DOING?

I'd be an ice cream scientist! (Yes, there is such a thing!) An ice cream scientist is responsible for researching, developing, and improving ice cream products. Talk about a dream job!

WHAT IS YOUR FAVORITE CAR?

That depends on who is driving. If I was with Helmut, Ferrari. For me, Mercedes.

WHAT'S YOUR FAVORITE PIECE OF JEWELRY?

Anything my husband gave me. He had the best taste and was always so generous.

WHAT IS YOUR FAVORITE BODY PART?

My eyes and my skin

IF YOU HAD TO CHANGE YOUR FIRST NAME, WHAT WOULD YOU CHANGE IT TO?

When I was in college, my friends and I would play a game while waiting for the cafeteria to open. We would line up and imagine our fictitious stage names and then set them to music. Mine was Desiree Lucci, sung to the tune of "Bésame Mucho." What can I say, we were very hungry, tired college girls passing the time waiting for the cafeteria to open.

WHAT IS YOUR FAVORITE TYPE OF WEATHER?

Low eighties and sunny with just the right amount of humidity to make my hair perfect.

WHAT IS THE BEST ONE-WORD INSULT?

Nothing is more satisfying than the real thing—so when I am really, *really* mad, my favorite curse word would be the f-bomb.

WHAT IS YOUR FAVORITE STORE?

Bergdorf Goodman

WHAT TIME DO YOU USUALLY WAKE UP IN THE MORNING?

Six a.m.

WHAT TIME DO YOU USUALLY GO TO BED AT NIGHT?

Too late to get up at six—usually around eleven p.m.

DESCRIBE YOUR STYLE IN ONE WORD.

Classic

WHAT WERE YOU AFRAID OF AS A CHILD?

The dark

WHAT'S SOMETHING YOU WOULD LIKE TO LEARN?

To speak Italian

WHAT IS A GOOD SPY CODE NAME FOR YOU?

Susie Q

WHAT DO YOU COLLECT?

China and crystal

WHAT IS YOUR FAVORITE TYPE OF STATIONERY?

Cartier note cards

WHAT IS YOUR FAVORITE THING TO DO IN THE SUMMERTIME?

Anything on the beach

WHAT IS ONE OF YOUR NICKNAMES?

Susie, which started when Helmut and I were first dating. Of course, he didn't always call me by name—usually "honey," "baby," and so on. I can't say whether Helmut was the impetus of this or not, but a few people on *All My Children* also referred to me as Susie. Some still do.

WHAT IS THE STUPIDEST DARE YOU EVER AGREED TO?

To go water skiing in a bikini. Lesson learned!

WHAT ITEM IS WORTH SPENDING MORE MONEY ON?

Anything classic that will stand the test of time

IS YOUR BED MADE RIGHT NOW?

Yes

HAVE YOU EVER WRITTEN A SONG FOR SOMEONE?

Yes, for my daughter, Liza, when she was a baby. I'd sing it to her at bedtime. This started around the time she was two or three years old. Liza was in a phase where she often said, "Mommy, I can do this by myself!" The song went like this: *One day while I was walking, my mommy and daddy too, I bought myself a beautiful balloon, and it was blue . . .*

WHAT IS ONE THING YOU REGRET SPENDING MONEY ON?

Buying anything I thought was quality that didn't last or that broke right away.

WHAT MOVIE DO YOU ENJOY QUOTING THE MOST?

Casablanca—"Here's looking at you, kid."

WHAT DISH DO YOU COOK BEST?

Spaghetti sauce

WHAT IS YOUR HIDDEN TALENT?

I have double-jointed fingers.

WHAT IS YOUR FAVORITE BOARD GAME?

Clue—I like all the little weapons.

WHAT IS YOUR FAVORITE RAINY-DAY ACTIVITY?

Getting organized. I always fantasize that I will curl up and read a good book by the fireplace, but . . . that doesn't happen. I use the time to get organized.

WHO IS YOUR FAVORITE DISNEY CHARACTER?

The entire cast of *Frozen* (the animated film)

FINISH THE PHRASE "THE WAY TO MY HEART IS . . ."

Humor, confidence, strength, authenticity, and, yes, food

WHAT ARE YOU MOST LOOKING FORWARD TO?

More travel—visiting Zürich, Paris, and London again, and so many new places I've never been to.

Chapter Twenty:
YOU DON'T MOVE ON, YOU MOVE FORWARD

The world breaks everyone and afterward
many are strong at the broken places.
—**ERNEST HEMINGWAY,** *A Farewell to Arms*

I know now that life inevitably weaves sadness into its fabric, a truth that touches every story and every journey. Yet I think it's vital not to let this sorrow take root, building walls around my heart. Sorrow will visit. But I don't want it to harden me or steal my capacity to love, dream, and find joy. Instead, I have learned that it is part of our humanity, and as awful as loss and sorrow are, they have deepened my compassion and profound gratitude for the moments of life that follow.

After Helmut passed, I did my best not to be a Debbie Downer with my friends. I never wanted to be a burden to anyone. Many times I found myself feeling out to sea—an expression that my godson, Tyler, articulated to me. In the beginning, I would rarely reach out to anyone to share what I was going through, let alone ask for help if I needed it. Frankly, asking for anything is not in my nature. I feel so fortunate to have a number of dear friends I feel comfortable doing that with, but it has taken me some time to feel that I could. I never wanted to appear needy or like I was somehow taken over by my sadness—even if I was.

A few months after losing my husband, I came across a TED Talk by writer and podcaster Nora McInerny, who shared what she learned about life and death after losing her unborn child, her dad, and then her husband within two months during 2014. The way she speaks so openly about it is both devastating and unexpectedly empowering. I love that she uses humor in equal measure with her incredible wisdom. I really appreciate that.

I learned when someone you love dies, people are well intentioned. They want to say and do the right thing, and they often do. However, it's also true that sometimes they don't. After Helmut passed, I didn't make any judgment about how people reacted. One friend in particular would have given the shirt off his back if you needed it. He was colorful, warm, and all around fabulous. He and Helmut had been like brothers. But when somebody in their circle passed away, he could not go to the funeral. He just couldn't handle it. Maybe it hit too close to home or made him think about his own mortality. Whatever the reasons, I understood and didn't feel hurt by his absence. I had empathy for how he might have felt.

Another well-intentioned thing people sometimes say is "Move on." As in, "It's time to move on." When you experience loss in your life, it's not like the curtain falls, and it's all done.

That's it.

The show is over.

No.

Absolutely not.

Helmut was and remains such a big part of who I am. How could I ever just . . . *move on*?

I see Helmut in our children and their children. I feel Helmut all around me. The memories, the absolute collection of a lifetime together, make up the pieces of my life.

So why would I ever want to leave that behind and move on?

I wouldn't.

The title of Nora's TED Talk just hit me as so very true:

"We don't 'move on' from grief. We move forward with it."

Wow.

This simple and very powerful message spoke to my heart and resonated in every fiber of my being.

It's so interesting how the right words can, and often do, come at the right time, even if they're from very unexpected places and people. I love that Nora's mission in life now is to make people comfortable with the uncomfortable, and let's face it, grief is uncomfortable . . . for everyone.

Grief is a beast.

I have never used the word *sucks* in my life, but there is no better way to say it—Helmut's passing sucks. If you really love the person you're with, that's the only word to describe this kind of loss. It sucks.

I truly believe in the promise of what lies ahead. It's now been a little more than three years since Helmut passed, and each day gets a little easier to breathe, to laugh, to live. This optimism is what keeps me moving forward, filling my heart with hope and anticipation for the future. It's a quality I deeply cherish and admire in others—those who, no matter what they've endured, continue to face the world with unwavering hope and positivity. Their ability to find light in every situation inspires me to hold on to that same spirit of hopefulness and my pursuit of being happy. And for the most part, I have a happy life, one for which I am so very grateful. In fact, with every passing day, I do find myself moving forward and toward a happier and more hopeful place.

> You can't change what happened. So have a little wallow, feel very sorry for yourself, and then get up and move forward.
>
> **—JOAN RIVERS**

I worried that writing this book would send a message of sadness. And I certainly didn't want this book to be sad. Yes, there's a chunk of it that has to do with loss and grieving, but that wasn't my reason for writing it. Rather, I hope that anyone who has gone through grieving, or is still going through grieving, will not feel alone. If my story can help someone know their experience is shared, then I consider that a win for both of us.

While, on some level, I wish we could all be spared grief, that would mean we never loved or never were loved. And because I do so believe in love, I wish instead that when you encounter grief, you find the best way for *you* to move forward—you find your joy and shine your brightest once again.

That's exactly what I've been doing.

Recently, I accepted a role in the film *Outcome*, cowritten and directed by Jonah Hill. When I first received the script, the role I was being offered frightened me. It was a challenge and definitely outside of my comfort zone. What a gift this was, and how very appreciative I was knowing I could do it. It's one thing to think you can do something, to accept the challenge of it. It's another thing to have done it and have the deep satisfaction of knowing you could. It gave me back my confidence—and it fueled my soul. I'm so grateful to Jonah, who sought me out for this role, and to Keanu Reeves, who was such a wonderful actor to perform with. I can't wait for you to see it.

As I was writing this book, I said yes to another challenging role, a performance comedy written by Joy Behar called *My First Ex-Husband*. Once again, I've taken a leap of faith in my growth, pushing my own limits and enjoying every moment. Doing this show was a first for me. It was my first time appearing off-Broadway and my first time doing this type of performance—a combination of stand-up comedy and character study. And boy, was I lucky! I had great material based on true stories Joy Behar had been collecting for years. And I was working with Judy Gold, who gave a master class on stand-up during every performance. Tonya Pinkins, a Tony winner, who was a fellow castmate of mine on *All My Children* playing the strong lawyer Olivia Frye, brought her sense of humor and experience and dynamic energy into the theater every single show. And the lovely Veanne Cox, an Emmy- and Tony-nominated actress and former ballet dancer, also brought her unique combination of elegance and humor to every performance.

Just as with *Outcome*, doing *My First Ex-Husband* gave me confidence. Evolving in my career and my life is so exciting. Each new challenge becomes an opportunity to learn, adapt, and stretch my wings. I've been stepping outside my comfort zone (in a good way), trusting that I am capable of more than I even knew.

While stepping out can feel intimidating, I am so grateful for the opportunities that have come my way. I am so happy that I have taken on these new challenges. When doubt was creeping in, I was very thankful that I could overcome it by digging deep and tapping into my determination, courage, and desire to move forward—and have a great time doing it.

LETTER TO MY YOUNGER SELF

Tell me, what is it you plan to do
with your one wild and precious life?
—MARY OLIVER, "The Summer Day"

Just as I was putting the finishing touches on this book, I went to see the spectacular Sarah Snook in *The Picture of Dorian Gray* on Broadway. I was invited to meet Sarah after the show and was thrilled to share with her how wonderfully powerful her performance was. When I was leaving, I was escorted out of the theater by walking across the stage. This was rather unusual, given there were many other exits I could have been taken to. As I entered the stage, there, right in front of me, was the ghost light. It took my breath away. I don't believe there are any coincidences in life—I think that everything happens for a reason. As I stood on that stage, staring out into the empty theater, I felt the same compelling emotion as when I stood on the empty stage when I was in college, and in this moment, I was both me today and that wide-eyed girl full of hopes and dreams—and determination. If I could go back in time, I wondered, what would I say to *her*? And then, it came to me. Write her a letter. So here goes.

Dear brand-new college graduate Susan,

First of all, God got it right. The Golden Rule is the best: Treat people as you would like to be treated. Remember to say thank you. You have been very blessed. Remember to give back. It is important for you to be in touch with how lucky you are, and showing your gratitude is respectful to the people you are saying it to. Acknowledge their talent, grace, generosity, and sharing. Remain grateful, even when life doesn't always feel fair.

I want to say to you, aim high—because, believe me, whether you realize it or not, you've got it. You've got great instincts, you've got talent, you've had great teachers, and you've got a great work ethic—you are the whole package. Remember that. As Dad taught us, never be afraid to raise your hand and ask questions. Do not be afraid! Forget your shyness. Don't allow that to hold you back from going after your dreams. And don't ever let anyone tell you that you can't achieve your goals. Keep your eyes and your ears open. Never lose your sense of wonder. So much of life is a collaboration; be a team player. Dream big and remember to enjoy the ride. Keep learning, keep growing always. This will serve you very well. Keep that fire in your belly and eliminate that negative inner monologue we all seem to have. We are all our own worst critics, but try to be your own best friend.

When it comes to love, follow your instincts (they are good ones) and lead with your heart, but keep your head on your shoulders—this is not always easy to do. Try to stay carefree as long as you can.

Drink Russian.

Drive German.

Wear Italian.

Kiss French.

Love,

Susan

ACKNOWLEDGMENTS

First, I must thank my dear friend Nelson DeMille, who encouraged me to write this book. He introduced me to the esteemed Sally Richardson, who, much to my surprise, had read my first book, and she, too, believed I had a second one in me. Hearing this from such esteemed publishing legends meant the world to me—and it also gave me the courage to move forward and take that leap of faith.

If I were going to do this, I knew I wanted to get the original book team back together. With Nelson's encouragement, that began with Laura Morton. Laura was my coauthor on *All My Life*, so I knew I would be in the very best hands. Thank you, Laura, for your incredible ability to capture my story and my voice, and for your guidance along the way. And thank you to Adam Mitchell, the behind-the-scenes guy who helped us seamlessly move through this process.

I also want to thank the fabulous Hope Innelli, whom I had also worked with as my editor on *All My Life*. Hope has a remarkable way of taking our writing and making it sing. Hope, you are the consummate professional, so outstanding at what you do, and so caring.

And to Jessica Sciacchitano, my treasured and tireless publicist, and her agency 2PM Sharp, for her support, her guidance, and her ability to achieve our goals. She really knows how to get things done. And she does it with so much grace and expertise.

To my publishing team at Blackstone: Josh Stanton, Anthony Goff, Rick Bleiweiss (who was responsible for acquiring this book), Greg Boguslawski, Anne Fonteneau, Megan Bixler, Josie Woodbridge, Stephanie Stanton, Kathryn English, Bryan Barney, Rachel Sanders, Sarah Bonamino, Rebecca Malzahn, and Candice Roditi—thank you all for your incredible belief in this book and your creative support.

To my literary agent, Mel Berger, and my attorney, Bill Sobel—thank you for your stellar advice and for navigating this project from start to finish. I couldn't have done it without you.

To Helene LiPuma, my longtime personal assistant, my "mission control." Your contributions to this process and everything I do are immeasurable. I am so grateful for your friendship and your loving care.

And to my beloved Frida, who passed away during the course of writing this book. You are sunshine and will forever hold such an important place in my heart and my life. I could never have been a working mom without you.

To all of my beloved friends who have stood by my side, I am eternally grateful for all of you. I could not have gotten through the past several years without your love and laughter and friendship. Thank you for holding me up when I wasn't sure I could stand on my own.

And finally, to each and every one of you reading this book: Thank you for your unwavering passion and for always supporting me for so many years. I am forever grateful for your presence, whether in person or from afar. Please know that I feel your love and enthusiastic support. You are the BEST!

NOTES

1 Maya Angelou, quoted in "Oprah's 2020 Vision Tour Visionaries: Tina Fey Interview," January 11, 2020, posted January 15, 2020, by Weight Watchers, YouTube, 9:48, https://www.youtube.com/watch?v=AiuLzhbvKs4.

2 American Heart Association, "The Facts About Women and Heart Disease," Go Red for Women, accessed May 9, 2025, https://www.goredforwomen.org/en/about-heart-disease-in-women/facts.

3 American Heart Association, "The Facts About Women."

4 American Heart Association, "The Facts About Women."

5 American Heart Association, "Greater Investment in Women's Heart Disease Research Could Yield Big Payoff," Go Red for Women, October 25, 2021, https://www.goredforwomen.org/en/about-heart-disease-in-women/latest-research/womens-research-funding.

6 Rose Kennedy, "JFK Assassination: Kennedy's Mother Rose's 'Agony' after Loss of Her Son, 60 Years Ago," posted November 22, 2023, by BBC News, YouTube, 2:18, https://www.youtube.com/watch?v=_3mVpS10uLg.

7 David Kessler, "David Kessler on the '6 Elements' of Good Grief," posted June 4, 2023, by The Grief Channel, YouTube, https://www.youtube.com/watch?v=OcwTl-2-ZHA.